नैनं छिन्दन्ति शस्त्राणि नैनं दहति पावकः।
न चैनं क्लेदयन्त्यापो न शोषयति मारुतः॥

Nainam chhindanti shastrani nainam dahati pavakaha,
Na chainam kledayantyapo na shoshayati marutaha.

Translation

No weaponry can cut it into parts, neither
can it be burned by flames,
Nor it can be soaked by water, or dried
by the winds . . . (the soul is immortal).
                    —*Bhagavad Gita (Chapter 2, Verse 23)*

GODS

OF

HINDUISM

A JOURNEY
INTO DIVINITY

MANHAR SHARMA

FiNGERPRINT!

Published by

FiNGERPRINT!
Prakash Books

Fingerprint Publishing
@FingerprintP
@fingerprintpublishingbooks
www.fingerprintpublishing.com

Copyright © 2025 Prakash Books
Copyright Text © Manhar Sharma

ISBN: 978 93 6214 417 1

CONTENTS

AUTHOR'S NOTE

The sight of Hindus worshiping many gods—each with unique and distinctive representations—may seem puzzling to those who are not familiar with their practices. These deities may have multiple arms, ride mystical creatures, rest on a serpent, wear tiger skin, have a necklace of skulls or even have an elephant head, among other unusual forms. Additionally, it can be challenging to grasp the diversity within the religion, which includes numerous sampradayas or sub-branches, gods, idols, saints, festivals, colors, sacred animals, symbols, practices and rituals. Despite these complexities, Hinduism, one of the oldest religions in the world, remains remarkably adaptive and dynamic by constantly transforming and evolving. This capacity to change and the ability to grow makes the ancient religion of Hinduism perpetually young. It is unique and at the same time cohesive, offering a rich tapestry of spiritual teachings that encompasses all aspects of life and dharma. This tradition offers a clear framework for understanding the universe, human life and the path to spiritual fulfillment.

Gods of Hinduism aims to simplify, interpret and categorize Hindu gods/deities and divine figures. The insights presented here are based on my finite knowledge and familiarity with the religion. Much of the literature in Hinduism is transmitted orally, incorporating diverse versions and legends that may sometimes be challenging to verify. The views and information expressed in this book are not intended as expert knowledge, nor are they meant to offend any religion, ethnic group, organization or individual. These reflections are offered in a spirit of positivity and should be received accordingly.

In the Spirit of Dharma!
Manhar Sharma
January 2025

PREFACE

The world has always revered Hinduism, not merely as a religion but also as an intersection of philosophy, spirituality and mythology. Whether for self-realization, healing or spirituality, Hinduism has never forced Sanatan Dharma on anyone. Hinduism respects all other religions in the world and believes that all faiths lead to the same God. This ensures Hinduism's commitment to religious liberty. Despite numerous outside influences and invasions, it has survived as a faith for thousands of years.

Today, Hinduism is the third-largest religion in the world. Other religions, such as Christianity, Islam, Judaism, Zoroastrianism, etc., believe that there is only one eternal God. Hinduism is an uncommon religion with hundreds of gods, deities, demigods, sacred symbols, divine diagrams and religious icons. At the same time, it also believes in the existence of the omnipresent God, who is everywhere—not only in idols but in all creations, including our very souls. In the Hindu pantheon, every god and goddess has different legends associated with them. Some are deemed more significant than others, based on their powers and abilities. Therefore, the concept of gods adhered to in Hinduism is unprecedented.

It would not be wrong to conclude that Hinduism is polytheistic because it worships countless deities, and the supreme gods that manifest in three forms: Lord Brahma—the creator, Lord Vishnu—the sustainer and Lord Shiva—the destroyer. At the same time, it supports monotheism, as it embraces the concept of the one Supreme God called Brahman, also referred to as Parmatman. The origins of Hindu gods are connected to the preliminary ancient Vedas, where the underlying concept further supports henotheism, which adheres to the worship of a single God while accepting the possible existence of other deities and demigods.

The study of the Hindu gods is eternally fascinating, but at the same time, it is a complex theology. It is not straightforward because of the variety in narratives and symbolism. Hinduism worships nature, many elements of life and numerous gods. Gods appear in the lore depending on the needs and requirements of the people and have been revered in distinct forms. These gods are incarnated across several sects of Hinduism. Consequently, they create a complex composition—an intricate structure. For instance, whenever we think of Hindu gods, the triad of Lord Brahma, Lord Vishnu and Lord Shiva comes to mind. There are many incarnations of Vishnu, including the legendary avatars of Lord Rama and Lord Krishna. Many gods come from Lord Shiva's family, including Lord Ganesha, Goddess Parvati, and his various forms like the lingam, Lord Nataraja, Lord Ardhanarishvara and Pancha-mukhalinga.

Next in the pantheon are Goddess Saraswati, the goddess of knowledge; Lord Vishwakarma, the god of engineering; Lord Jagannath, the god of the universe; Lord Kubera and Goddess Lakshmi, the god and goddess of wealth; Shitala Mata, the goddess associated with smallpox; and Oladevi, the goddess revered in relation to cholera. Following them are Lord Hanuman; Lord Shakti; Lord Agni, the god of fire; Lord Surya, the sun god; along with sacred trees like pipal, banyan, tulsi and neem. The list extends to include Manasa Devi, the goddess of snakes; Lord Khatu Shyam; Lord Shaligram Shila; sacred rivers like the Ganga; the nine planets in the universe, including Lord Rahu and Lord Ketu; animals such as the cow and celestial birds like Garuda; and sacred symbols like Aum, Swastika, Shri Yantra and many more.

In this book, I have categorized gods and deities based on their similarities and the frequency of their appearances in Hindu lore. This approach is essential for understanding how the religion connects different gods and practices. It helps explore how these gods relate to each other, how they are worshiped and how they guide one spiritually and in everyday life. Accordingly, the categorization of gods and deities based on their similarities and prevalence in Hinduism is as follows:

Vedic Gods: Due to the limited number of Vedic scriptures available today, we do not know the exact number of ancient gods worshiped during the Vedic period. However, there are approximately 33 significant deities—each with their unique narrative and symbolism. While some gods from the Vedic period are forgotten, others continue to be worshiped in modern Hinduism. The latter category includes Lord Surya; Lord Agni; Lord Yama, the god of death; and others.

Puranic Gods: The list of gods in this category is extensive, drawn from the Puranas and epics such as the Ramayana and the Mahabharata. The Puranas are anonymous manuscripts that have been read by numerous sages since ancient times. There are 18 Mahapuranas and Upapuranas each. They consist of more than 400,000 verses. They predominantly revolve around the Hindu trinity of Lord Brahma, Lord Vishnu and Lord Shiva, along with their respective consorts. They also praise the various avatars of Lord Vishnu and the family members of Lord Shiva, illuminating the complex relationships and rich stories associated with these deities.

Nature and Celestial Gods: This category includes sacred trees, plants, rivers, planets and heavenly bodies. This diverse category of gods is worshiped in modern Hinduism. Small offerings are presented to these deities during all prominent festivals.

Tutelary and Folk Gods: This category includes demigods worshiped by various local communities. The gods in this section are adored by a few people from specific sects, villages or regions. Sometimes, evil demigods are also made a part of this category.

Ancestors or Spirits: Worshiping ancestors has been an essential part of Hinduism. The rituals performed for ancestors are crucial—they express unconditional love, faith and reverence toward a person's forbears. In ancient texts, Agni Yagna or the fire sacrifice and offerings are stated as debts that every individual owes to their deceased parents and ancestors.

Devils and Demons: In Hinduism, both the gentle and generous Goddess Parvati as well as her fierce and tantric manifestation, Goddess Kali, are worshiped and adored. Since the Vedic period, demons, devils and evil forces have existed in Hindu beliefs. Demons are occasionally revered, as they are believed to have the power to cause destruction or bring bad luck. These beings and similar power-seeking clans related to the more benevolent devas have been added to the list of gods and goddesses in the Hindu pantheon.

Symbols, Yantras and Diagrams: Lastly, like any other religion, Hinduism has adopted many holy and spiritual emblems derived from the scriptures, the culture and ancient folklore. Some of the most pious and revered representations are Aum, Swastika, Shri Chakra, or more popularly Shri Yantra and Bindu.

Millions of Hindus worldwide worship these gods and goddesses in countless temples, idols and artworks. Men, women and children bow with folded hands in reverence to these divine figures, who are believed to have descended to the world through various avatars and manifestations.

I hope this book offers a comprehensive overview of the extensive Hindu pantheon, presented in a structured and accessible way. It aims to provide insights into the diverse and intricate nature of these deities, highlighting their significance within Hindu philosophy and culture. Ultimately, the true measure of this book's success would lie in its ability to inspire readers to delve deeper into the captivating and sacred realm of these gods. I encourage you to explore their stories, teachings and the rich cultural heritage they embody, as there is much to discover in this profound tradition.

On a further note, in this book's main body of text, I have chosen to limit the usage of titles such as 'Goddess' and

'Lord' before the names of gods and goddesses. Frequent use of these titles can interrupt the story, confuse readers and lead to misunderstandings about the significance of the gods. Therefore, while I deeply respect and fully recognize the importance of these deities, I wanted to focus on creating a smooth narrative flow, wherein the book's cohesive structure and overall readability would not get interrupted. I have instead highlighted the honorific titles in the book's chapter titles, headings and subheadings. This way, we can honor the significance of the gods, while keeping the narrative engaging.

INTRODUCTION
TO HINDUISM

ORIGIN OF HINDUISM

No ancient civilization in the world has existed without engaging in some form of religious practice. Every primitive society has had its own beliefs, such as establishing harmony with their land, honoring supernatural powers, performing sacrificial rituals, worshiping angels or demons, believing in the afterlife, etc. When we study the history of such ancient cultures, we do not find the exact dates of any events—and the only way to decipher the religious inclinations of such civilizations is with stone inscriptions, artifacts, preserved manuscripts and archaeological findings. Hinduism is an ancient religion too, but its origins appear to differ from other faiths in some marked ways. We cannot find a specific founder or event that marks the birth of Hinduism, unlike what has been observed in Christianity, Islam, Judaism, Zoroastrianism and Buddhism. Conversely, Hinduism's sacred texts were not discovered in written form, such as on carved stones or papyrus.

So, how was the knowledge preserved?

The wise seers in ancient times played a key role in keeping Hinduism's sacred heritage and spiritual knowledge alive. They memorized vast teachings, ensuring this wisdom was passed down accurately through generations. This knowledge included spiritual principles, rituals, hymns and philosophical insights—all shared orally from teacher to student. This oral tradition, marked by careful recitation and memorization, ensured the teachings' purity and preserved them over thousands of years. As time passed, enlightened sages organized and compiled these teachings into the Vedas, the foundational scriptures of Hinduism. By compiling these teachings, the sages ensured that the spiritual and cultural heritage of Hinduism was conserved for future generations, providing an organized and accessible collection of ancient wisdom.

So, how far back can we go to find traces of these sacred texts and teachings? And even then, can we determine the origin of Hinduism from them? The answers to these questions are doubtful, debatable and controversial. Hinduism has survived for thousands of years despite many invasions and influences. For over 5,000 years, the religion has embraced ideas and beliefs from all parts of the world. One of the oldest sacred scriptures of Hinduism, known as the Rigveda, states:

आ नो भद्राः क्रतवो यन्तु विश्वत्

Aa no bhadrah krtavo yantu vishvatah.

Translation

Let the noble thoughts come to me from all directions.

—*Rigveda (1.89.1)*

According to some Indian scholars, Hinduism began around 8000 BCE.[1] However, Western scholars propose that its inception happened toward the end of the prehistoric age in India, between 4000–1500 BCE.[2] Then again, many European scholars and historians who have studied Vedic literature, state that it is the Vedic period that marks the origin of Hinduism, which emerged during or shortly after the advent of the Indus Valley civilization.

Traces of this advanced civilization were found on the Indian subcontinent by archaeologists. The civilization was located on the banks of the Indus River, in modern-day Pakistan and northwest India. It is suggested by many academics that the riparian settlement started to diminish in the second millennium BCE. However, no substantial proof of the reasons for its decline exists to date. Archaeologists have given various reasons, such as climate change, the drying up of major rivers, invasions by the Aryans and natural disasters. Some historians have also hypothesized a pandemic as the cause of its collapse.

Various kinds of scientific and geographical research is still being employed to understand the origin of the Vedic age. One approach involves correlating the astronomical events mentioned in the Vedas, which note the planetary positions and alignments that have recurred across centuries. Based on certain characteristics, this period could range from 4000–2000 BCE.[3] Hence, any concrete conclusion about the origins of Hinduism, and the initial timeline of the religion, cannot be made.

Similarly, there can be a discrepancy in the names of the places mentioned in the Vedas, as names change every 100–200 years. And we are considering thousands of years and more—so there is a definite scope for errors. The seven rivers mentioned in the Vedas were also used to gauge the origin of the Vedic age. However, over thousands of years, rivers have also changed their course or dried up. For example, the most sacred river mentioned in the Vedas is the River Saraswati. Historians opine that the river did not exist until a few years ago. Geophysical researchers from the National Remote Sensing Centre (NRSC)/Indian Space Research Organisation (ISRO) studied the river and its passage and found that it had last flowed some 4,000 years ago. Therefore, there is no definite conclusion. Similarly, many other interpretations have been considered, but no substantial proof of the origin of Hinduism or the Vedic period has been obtained.[4] Despite the controversies, some scholars agree that the roots of Hinduism existed during or before the prehistoric period (the time in human history before writing was invented—in the Indian subcontinent, this period happened before the emergence of the Indus Valley civilization). Hence, the beginnings of Hinduism can be directly established through its relationship with the Vedas.

The Vedic age is divided into two parts: the pre-Vedic period and the post-Vedic period. Moreover, the Vedas were composed in one of the most pristine languages in the world, Vedic Sanskrit. According to ancient scriptures, the people who started practicing the Vedas were called Aryans. "Arya" means noble in Sanskrit. The term "Vedas" is derived from the Sanskrit word "vid," meaning knowledge. These sacred texts were written in Vedic Sanskrit, which is different from Classical Sanskrit. The former was the vernacular of that time, and the latter was its dialect. Additionally, Classical Sanskrit was standardized later.

Jews believe Hebrew to be the language of God. Arabs say Arabic is the language of God. Similarly, in Hinduism, Sanskrit is considered the language of the gods. It is referred to as Devbhasha or Devavani.

So, why is Sanskrit as a sacred language crucial to Hinduism?

Some exciting facts make Sanskrit unlike any other holy language. Before any other sacred or vernacular languages were formed, Sanskrit was widely availed in the Indian subcontinent. However, it is now spoken by a minority group only. Many Indian languages and the languages of some other countries are derived from or are directly influenced by Sanskrit. It is also known as the mother of several (but not all) Indian languages, in the same way that, say, languages like English, Spanish and French are derived from Latin. In the present day, Hindi is the most widely spoken language in India, and it is primarily derived from Prakrit, a medieval Indian vernacular that originated from Sanskrit.

Another interesting fact is that a few Sanskrit words are found in Latin as well, and many Western scholars acknowledge this. The impression of Hinduism and Sanskrit on the West was described by the author Will Durant as follows:

India was the motherland of our race, and Sanskrit the mother of Europe's languages, she was the mother of our philosophy; mother, through the Arabs, of much of our mathematics; mother, through the Buddha, of the ideals embodied in Christianity; mother, through the village community, of self-government and democracy. Mother India is, in many ways, the mother of us all.[5]

During the Vedic age, when most of the world's languages and phonological rules were nonexistent, the Vedas in India flourished with countless Sanskrit mantras. Since the Vedic period, the sounds of all vowels (svara) or base vowels (a), and consonants (vyanjana) in Sanskrit have been precisely fixed. The language has not undergone any major change for centuries, especially since the scholar Panini laid down the ground rules in Ashtadhyayi. The words in Sanskrit still have the same pronunciation, sound and tone. Since the language is well-known in the modern world, neither the grammar nor the vowel systems have been modified.

Furthermore, Sanskrit is one of the most precise languages, with more than half a million words! These words have multiple forms and variations. New words can be created through compounding and derivation. Sanskrit has a robust root system, with over 2,000 roots that can be combined to form words. It also uses prefixes and suffixes to modify roots and create new words, increasing its vocabulary. One of the features that distinguishes the language is its ability to be spoken using the fewest of words. It has many such impressive characteristics, including the fact that all letters are formed using a uniform sound that the vocal cords initially make; one must combine precise lip movements, accurate tongue positioning, correct mouth shapes and controlled throat vibrations. These elements work together to form the unique and complex phonetic system of the language.

THE VEDAS

What are the Vedas? Why are they important? And how have they depicted Hinduism?

The Vedas are considered the earliest and most sacred of Hindu scriptures.[6] They are revered for their spiritual wisdom, dictates of rituals and insights into the nature of existence, which form the basis of Hindu religious and philosophical traditions. Their knowledge is deemed eternal and supreme. The Vedas comprise hymns, prayers, rituals and philosophical teachings passed down orally for generations, before they were written down. As per certain Hindu beliefs, when Brahma created the world, he gave all the knowledge to the great seers through the Vedas. This knowledge was transferred to the next generation and so on. Even today, most of the rituals and religious practices of the Vedas are relevant. These texts have significantly shaped Indian culture, influencing rituals, ethics and spiritual practices that continue to hold sway even today. Many of these rituals are conducted upon birth, marriage and death, and are based on Vedic doctrines. It can be said that the Vedas are the oldest sacred texts available to humankind.

अनन्ता वै वेदाः

Ananta vai Vedaah.

Translation

Vedas are endless and infinite.

—*Brihadaranyaka Upanishad (4.1.6)*

The Vedas have a legacy of thousands of years. There are no greater scriptures in Hinduism. Evidence of the Vedas can be found throughout all other Hindu scriptures. Their principles and practices are elaborated upon, interpreted and applied in other sacred texts, such as the Upanishads, Puranas, epics like the Mahabharata and Ramayana, and various shastras. The Vedas are considered to be anadi—which means they have no beginning or end; something that has always existed, even before the beginning of time. Hence, they are eternal.

Vedas are also called apaurusheya[7] which means "not created or composed by any person." The sacred texts of the Vedas are believed to have been created by Brahma, making their origin untraceable. Some mantras are attributed to different sages, implying that they composed them, which isn't entirely accurate. This concept is akin to assuming that Galileo was the first person to observe the sun and planets, introducing the solar system to the world, despite the sun existing long before humanity on Earth. Thus, while sages are associated with certain mantras, it suggests their recognition rather than authorship.

Other religious scriptures, such as the Puranas, the Bhagavad Gita and the epics, also mention the Vedas and their essence. The Bhagavad Gita is one of the most translated and published sacred scriptures in Hinduism. It means "the song of God."

In the Bhagavad Gita, Krishna says:

वेदानां समवेदोऽस्मि देवानामस्मि वासवः ।
इन्द्रियाणाममनश्चास्मि भूतानामस्मि चेतना ॥

Vedanam Samavedosmi Devanamasmi Vasavah,
Indriyanam Manas-chasmi Bhutanamasmi Chetana.

Translation

I am the Samaveda amongst all the Vedas,
I am Indra amongst all the celestial gods.
I am the mind among the senses,
and the consciousness of all beings.

—Bhagavad Gita (Chapter 7, Verse 22)

Similarly, the pranava or eternal sound "Om Tat Sat," has been used as the threefold manifestation of the supreme, absolute truth. At the time of creation, the Vedas and various sacrifices originated from it. The noble Veda Vyasa, the revered rishi who classified the Vedas, mentions the greatness of the texts in the Mahabharata. He says, "At the beginning of the universe, God created the divine Vedas, an illuminating voice for human beings."[8]

The Shastras—another revered text of Hinduism—assert that the Vedas are the words of God. Great scholars and reformers worldwide have reiterated that the Vedas are the most authoritative and important texts in Hinduism. In his address to the World Congress of Religions in 1893, Swami Vivekananda stated, "The Hindus have received their religion through the revelation of the Vedas."[9] He proudly added that Hinduism is the religion (or the only religion) that believes in the truth of all religions, as it states that in order to reach God, one can follow any path. Many other religions that emerged after Hinduism claimed that if one wanted to reach the divine, the only way was through a particular practice.

एकम् सत् विप्रा बहुधा वदन्ति

Ekam Sat Vipra Bahudha Vadanti.

Translation

Truth is one only, and people perceive
it differently, our God is one, but wise people call
it by different names or perceive him differently.

—*Rigveda (1.164.46)*

If anyone wants to acquire infinite knowledge of Hinduism, the Vedas are the ultimate source. They offer insight into the life during the Vedic period. The Vedas' essence is to regulate Hinduism's social, legal, domestic and religious customs. Hindus believe that the Vedas encapsulate eternal wisdom for various stages of life. They also contain hymns for praying to Vedic gods, such as Agni, the god of fire; Indra, the god of Heaven; Varuna, the god of water and sky; and Surya, the sun god. The Vedas are divided into four categories:

- Rigveda
- Samaveda
- Yajurveda
- Atharvaveda

Each of the Vedas can be further classified into Samhita, Brahmana, Aranyaka and Upanishad.

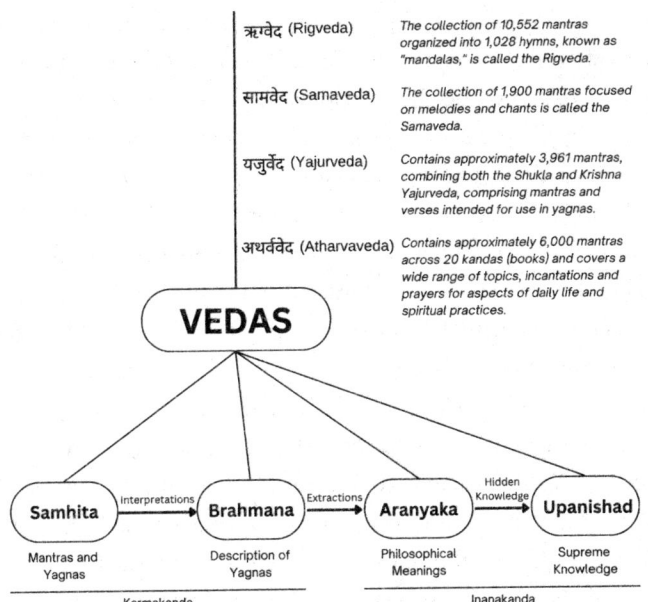

ऋग्वेद (Rigveda) — The collection of 10,552 mantras organized into 1,028 hymns, known as "mandalas," is called the Rigveda.

सामवेद (Samaveda) — The collection of 1,900 mantras focused on melodies and chants is called the Samaveda.

यजुर्वेद (Yajurveda) — Contains approximately 3,961 mantras, combining both the Shukla and Krishna Yajurveda, comprising mantras and verses intended for use in yagnas.

अथर्ववेद (Atharvaveda) — Contains approximately 6,000 mantras across 20 kandas (books) and covers a wide range of topics, incantations and prayers for aspects of daily life and spiritual practices.

VEDAS

Samhita — Interpretations → Brahmana — Extractions → Aranyaka — Hidden Knowledge → Upanishad

Mantras and Yagnas | Description of Yagnas | Philosophical Meanings | Supreme Knowledge

Karmakanda | Jnanakanda

The first part, called Samhita, contains verses, which are the core of the Vedas and consists mainly of mantras or incantations. The second part is the Brahmana, which interprets and comments on the mantras in the Samhita—this, in turn, helps understand the meaning and significance of the sacred text. The Brahmana provides a way of performing rituals called Karmakanda. The hymns of the Karmakanda group were used during yagnas and they provide detailed descriptions of these rites. Similarly, Jnanakanda, comprising the Aranyaka and the Upanishads, is the profound wisdom that delves into the intricate knowledge of the Vedas.

Aranyaka means "written in the forest." It is an extraction from the Brahmana. The Upanishads are extracted from Aranyaka[10] and is akin to seeking hidden knowledge. The

Aranyaka focuses on rituals and their symbolic meanings. Hence, they serve as a bridge between the ritualistic Brahmanas and the philosophical Upanishads. Intended for forest-dwelling hermits, it emphasizes meditation and inner contemplation. The Upanishads are primarily philosophical and metaphysical texts. They explore concepts such as the nature of reality, atman or the self and Brahman or the ultimate reality. They are considered the culmination of Vedic thought, focusing on spiritual knowledge and enlightenment. The quest to attain higher knowledge leads one to the Supreme Self and God[11]—such knowledge is available in the Upanishads.

The Rigveda is the oldest and most important scripture. It contains approximately 10,552 mantras organized into 1,028 hymns[12] across 10 different books, which are called mandalas. It is believed that the first and the tenth mandalas were added later, in the post-Vedic age. The Rigveda includes mantras for pleasing the Vedic gods, rituals for praising and worshiping them, sacred prayers for health, wealth and well-being, a philosophical review of the concepts of truth, and the origin of the universe, existence and nonexistence. It talks about the mind, vision, natural forces, rules of social life and rituals for weddings, wars, gifts and yagnas.

The Samaveda, known as the Veda of melodies or chants, originates from the Rigveda and is primarily composed of hymns arranged with musical notes. The melodies of Samaveda are sung during Vedic rituals, enriching the traditional recitations of the Rigveda with a melodic and rhythmic dimension. While its verses are derived from the Rigveda, the Samaveda is reorganized and adapted to fit the musical chants used in ceremonies, emphasizing its role in elevating the ritual experience through the power of sound and melody.

Next, the Yajurveda contains detailed instructions for performing rituals, including the correct procedures, mantras and offerings required to appease the deities and maintain cosmic order. It includes prose mantras and verses used by the hotri or priests during yagnas. These rituals involve elaborate ceremonies, such as offerings into the holy fire. The Yajurveda is divided into two main parts: Shukla Yajurveda or the White Yajurveda and Krishna Yajurveda or the Black Yajurveda.

Unlike the other Vedas, which predominantly explore ritualistic and philosophical themes, the Atharvaveda delves deep into the practical aspects of human life. Its verses offer guidance on rituals that address concerns such as health, protection and social harmony. The Atharvaveda enriches the Vedic canon by encompassing both spiritual and worldly dimensions, providing valuable insights into ancient Indian beliefs and practices that extend beyond traditional religious ceremonies.

***

In Hinduism, the two main categories of scriptures are Shruti and Smriti. Shruti in Sanskrit means "that which is heard and should be remembered." The scriptures are understood as God's words and should be remembered without being recorded in any form. Hence, since the very beginning, these scriptures have been heard, learned and transmitted from generation to generation. Rigveda, Samaveda, Yajurveda and Atharvaveda, along with the Samhita, Brahmana, Aranyaka and Upanishads, are called the sacred texts of Shruti. Other important Shruti scriptures are the Vedangas, which are the six auxiliary disciplines of Hinduism developed in ancient times, and the Upavedas, which are the texts on the Vedas' auxiliary themes.

On the other hand, Smriti refers to something that is remembered or is memory-based. In other words, it is the product of human intellect. The Smriti scriptures are the texts that the seers wrote in the later Vedic period. As opposed to Shruti, Smriti is a derivative work. Smriti texts were inspired by Shruti and are given lesser importance. These texts include Dharmasutra, popular sutras written by seers like Manu and Narad Muni, the 18 Puranas and Itihasas like the Ramayana, the Mahabharata or the Bhagavad Gita. Smriti texts structurally branched over time from the so-called "limbs of the Vedas." While most scholars accept Shruti's authority, many also deny its divinity. Of all the Shrutis, the Upanishads are the best known and are the spiritual core of Hinduism.

***

The Vedic scriptures have passed through centuries without the slightest alteration or adjustment. But how is that possible?

These scriptures and sacred texts are numerous in number. For example, the Rigveda alone will have shakhas or branches ranging from 5–21. Out of all the Rigveda's divisions, as mentioned in the scriptures, only one is available today. It is known as Shakala. The combined mantras found in the Rigveda are more than 10,500—in the present-day segregation of the Rigveda, which is based on the 10 different mandalas marked from 1–10. Considering this, the number of sacred scriptures and texts available during the ancient period must have been enormous.

So, how was it possible to memorize innumerable mantras or suktas with the correct sound, melody and tone in the ancient period? How did the seers and rishis pass down the sacred scriptures for centuries without any alteration or modification? It is almost impossible to consider this in the present day!

Moving on, the mantra *Vasudhaiva Kutumbakam*, appeared in the following verse:

अयं बन्धुरयं नेति गणना लघुचेतसाम्।
उदारचरितानां तु वसुधैव कुटुम्बकम्॥

Ayam bandhurayam neti ganana laghuchetasam,
Udaracharitanam tu vasudhaiva kutumbakam.

Translation

This person is a relative; that person is not.
Such calculations are for those with limited hearts
[narrow-minded people]. For those with noble
conduct, the whole world is one family.
—*Maha Upanishad (Chapter 6, Verse 72)*

Even a slight alteration in an accented syllable or tone will change the meaning of the sentence entirely. The United Nations Educational, Scientific and Cultural Organization (UNESCO) declared the oral tradition of the Vedas of India a "Masterpiece of the Oral and Intangible Heritage of Humanity."[13]

So, how did the ancient seers preserve these scriptures orally?

The seers used various types of recitation methods. Some of these techniques, still known to us, are called Padapatha. This recitation method was designed to memorize the scriptures, sacred texts and their pronunciation correctly, including the Vedic pitch and accent. Moreover, it also maintained the purity of the books. Some other recitation methods were Samhita,

Jata, Krama, Prakrati, Sikha, Rekha, Danda, Ratha, Dhwaja and Ghana. Some of these techniques are elaborated below:

Samhita Patha: In this method, syllables and complete mantras are chanted in their original form without any special patterns or alterations. The recitation maintains the original phonetic sound, tone and rules of chorus and intonation.

Jata Patha: In this method, every couple of adjoining shabdas or words in the mantras are first recited in their original sequence, then repeated in reverse and finally, again in the original sequence. This pattern continues throughout the mantra as each subsequent set of words is introduced.

Prakrati Patha: This method involves reciting with deliberate pauses after every few words or after encountering any special grammatical codes within the text. This method emphasizes the accurate pronunciation and restoration of each word in its originally intended form.

Despite modern technology and preservation techniques, few people can grasp and understand these scriptures. Most Hindus in the modern world only know the names of the four Vedas. Thanks to all the available sources, like books, stories from grandparents and television series, people know about the Bhagavad Gita, the Mahabharata and the Ramayana. There are also some paradoxes about why most people do not study the Vedas. Sometimes, they find these scriptures difficult to comprehend and assume that only great gurus or Sanskrit scholars can understand them. Sometimes, it is boring as they talk about God, nature, karma or acts and deeds, Brahman, atman, samsara, reincarnation, social obligations, moksha and eternal life. They also question our true selves and the purpose of life.

But have people ever pondered about the profound wisdom that lies within the Vedas and Upanishads?

THE VEDIC
PANTHEON

To understand Hinduism comprehensively, it is also essential to explore the diverse representations of Hindu gods through their idols. These idols depict gods, goddesses, deities, demigods, sacred animals and sages. Crafted from stone, wood, clay, marble or metals, every idol embodies specific qualities, stories and attributes associated with the deity they represent. They play a profound role in Hindu traditions, showcasing the variety of practices for worship. Studying these idols offers insights into the roles and importance of Hindu gods in rituals and daily worship. Moreover, exploring these idols deepens one's understanding of Hindu cosmology, ethics and the cultural contexts of deity veneration. Idols of Hindu gods are like physical doors that open the pathway to understanding and admiring the various facets of the religion.

Many religions perceive idol worship as an act of superstition. However, Hinduism accepts idol worship as an expression of faith, love and connection to God. Foreign invaders have desecrated and vandalized Hindu idols and temples since the early medieval period, but the Hindu community has shown remarkable resilience and steadfastness in facing such challenges. The right place to begin this study is with Hinduism's primal gods: the Vedic gods. Even though we do not find many indicators of divine entities in the Vedas, the deities depicted in these texts are known as the Vedic gods. All the information obtained about the Vedic gods and goddesses is inherited from the Vedas. They were the foundational gods of Hinduism. Vedic gods had a significant influence on the modern gods of the religion.

Most of the Vedic yagnas, performed to appease the Vedic gods, were meant to achieve the goals of human life, including karma, dharma, artha and moksha. Some Vedic gods are still worshiped in households and temples during festivals and rituals in modern Hinduism. Due to the limited number of Vedic scriptures available today, we do not know the exact number of gods worshiped during the ancient period. Nevertheless, approximately 33 major deities are identified in the Vedas, each with their unique narrative and attributed symbolisms.

They are commonly called devas or devatas, and are not meant to represent the Supreme God. Some devas manifest as the Supreme God's glory, and are categorized into eight Vasus, eleven Rudras and twelve Adityas, including Indra and Prajapati. The Vedic gods can be further divided into major and minor gods. Hence, major gods in the Vedic age were Indra; Surya; Agni; Varuna; Yama; Vishwakarma and Soma, the god of plants. Furthermore, the minor Vedic gods included Ushas, goddess of dawn; Ashvins, the twin Vedic gods; Dyaus, god of the sky; and many more. Most of the gods from the Vedic period are forgotten, and only a few of them—like Surya, Agni and Yama—are worshiped in modern Hinduism.

The method of worship during the Vedic period is distinct from the practices in modern Hinduism. In the Vedic period, venerating the gods mostly includes a purification ceremony called havana or yagna, an offering ritual. This yagna is an act of offering gratitude to a god by making sacrifices to the fire god.

According to some scholars, idolatry was not common in the Vedic period. But a yagna is described more than 1,184 times and was a common practice. There is no major Hindu ceremony that does not include an offering to Agni. However, new deities emerged and gained prominence in the later post-Vedic era.

It will not be possible to include all the Vedic gods in this book as there are hundreds of Vedic gods and seers that exist in the texts—each with different or similar legends. However, I have included some of the most important deities who were widely worshiped in the Vedic age.

LORD INDRA
From the Greatest Vedic Deity to Sly King

Indra was one of the most notable gods during the Vedic period. With around 1,028 hymns in the Rigveda ascribed to him, he was the most preferred deity. Indra played a crucial role as the guardian deity in the Vedic age, as he is the god of storm and thunder. It is important to note that Indra is also infamously called "the thousand-eyed." During the Vedic period, Indra was considered the epitome of strength and courage. Additionally, his wife, Indrani, also known as Shachi, was revered for her unwavering loyalty and devotion. Together, they were seen as the ultimate power couple.

Furthermore, a specific animal or bird is associated with each Hindu deity, which serves as the vahana or the deity's vehicle for travel. Airavata, the White Elephant, is Indra's vahana. It was the Samudra Manthan or the churning of the ocean that produced the magnificent Airavata.

Indra is the son of Heaven's father, Dyaus Pita, and Mother Earth, Prithivi. Indra's twin brother is Agni. Indra is mostly illustrated as a god with four arms, riding a white elephant. In one hand, he holds his weapon, the Vajra, and in another, either a conch shell or a bow and arrow. Sometimes, he even holds a hook and a net. In certain later scriptures, particularly the Puranas, there are indications that Indra's throne was occupied by different deities during various periods of the Vedic age, along with references that allude to the shifting power among them. This implies that there were likely different versions of Indra at different times throughout the Vedic era.

The most famous tale involving Indra, the king of the devas, is his epic battle with Vritra, who was a mighty asura with the power to withhold the world's waters, causing severe drought and suffering for all living beings. He hoarded the celestial waters, preventing rain and the flow of rivers, leading to widespread distress. To end Vritra's tyranny, Indra, as the god of thunder, rain and Heaven, decided to confront him. The devas bestowed Indra with immense strength and weapons, including the powerful thunderbolt, Vajra, which was created by the blessed Vishwakarma from the bones of Dadhichi, a revered sage.

In the later Vedic period, there was a shift in the worship of Indra, who was no longer revered as he was before. Instead, he was seen as the god of rain and the Guardian of the East. Indra's reputation changed significantly over time. He was associated with apsaras, the celestial dancing spirits of Svarga or Heaven, and was sometimes depicted as fond of drinking the intoxicating drink, soma. On the other hand, according to various Puranic scriptures, he even became jealous of humans worshiping other gods. It is interesting to see how Indra, once celebrated for his strength and courage, came to be portrayed as untrustworthy, lazy and even a daydreamer, as the Puranic gods gained more prominence, eventually causing the decline of the Vedic gods' power and reverence.

In addition, in some stories, Indra is presented as an infamous king. He feared losing his throne to someone more pious, dominant and deserving. Other tales tell us that an insecure Indra was ready to go to any lengths to save his throne.

These legends are narrated a bit differently in the Mahabharata.

There is an anecdote about Indra's intoxication that after drinking soma, he attempted to seduce Ahalya, the wife of the rishi, Gautama. Consequently, Indra was cursed by the rishi for having an affair with his wife. In another story, a rishi named Vishwamitra frightened all the gods and attempted to create another Svarga. Scared by Vishwamitra's powers, Indra sent the apsara Menaka, who was created during the Samudra Manthan, to seduce him and interrupt his meditation. Possessing quick intelligence, she was one of the most beautiful apsaras. However, she fell in love with Vishwamitra. The apsara gave birth to a girl who grew up in the ashram of a sage named Kanva. She came to be known as Shakuntala. It is believed that Shakuntala fell in love with King Dushyanta and gave birth to Bharata. King Bharata was the founder of the Kuru dynasty in the epic, Mahabharata.

There is another important story about Indra, which involves a young Krishna, an avatar of Vishnu, who persuaded the villagers of Vrindavan to worship the Govardhana Hill instead of Indra. Angered by this, Indra unleashes a devastating storm on the village. Consequently, Krishna lifts the Govardhana Hill with his little finger to protect the villagers, providing shelter for seven days and nights. Realizing Krishna's divine power, Indra ceases the storm and humbly seeks his forgiveness and acknowledges his supremacy. This story highlights devotion, humility and the importance of nature. Additionally, Indra is depicted as Bali's father in the Ramayana and as Arjuna's father in the Mahabharata.

From most of the post-Vedic period legends, it was evident that Indra had descended to an inferior position. Nevertheless, he is still worshiped in some parts of India,

Thailand and Sri Lanka. Indra-like figures also appear in many other mythologies and religions. In Greek mythology, Indra is compared with Zeus. There are many vague similarities between them. Both are considered the king of gods. Their armaments, thunderbolt and the Vajra, are similar; both have also slaughtered sea monsters. Indra's opponent was the asura serpent, Vritra, and Zeus conquered Typhon, the monstrous serpentine giant. Similarly, Jupiter, the god of the sky and thunder from Roman mythology shares the same attributes. Moreover, like Indra, there are gods in Buddhism, Jainism and Zoroastrianism that also share the same characteristics and have comparable mythological tales.

LORD SURYA
The Visible and Invisible Form

A solar deity has been worshiped in different forms in almost all the recorded religions across ancient civilizations. In ancient Egypt, the solar deity is represented by the sun god Ra, who rides a "Sun Boat". There was a significant sun worship tradition in the Mesopotamian civilization as well. Similarly, in Greek mythology, Helios is the prominent sun god. He was believed to have driven a golden chariot that would carry the sun across the skies daily. The Colossus of Rhodes was an enormous bronze statue of Helios and was one of the old Seven Wonders of the World.

Another example is in the Roman civilization, where one of the major festivals, the Winter Solstice, was celebrated as the sun's rebirth. Later, this festival was replaced in Christianity by the birth of Christ. Likewise, if we study Buddhist cosmology, Chinese mythology or any other theology, almost all have worshiped the sun god in one form or another. In a similar vein, Hinduism's worship of the sun is also truly inspiring.

In Hinduism, the sun is one of the most powerful Vedic gods. The sun is the only god that can be seen and worshiped daily. He has several names, but Surya and Savitr are frequently used in the Vedas. Scholars say Surya is for worshiping the Sun's visible form, and Savitr is for its invisible state. In Hindu scriptures, Savitr means "the one who creates." He is portrayed as riding a chariot driven by seven horses. The golden-eyed Savitr has four golden hands and a body that is red in color. He carries a lotus, which symbolizes life, along with a shankha or conch, a chakra or discus, and a gada or mace. His chariot with seven horses has 12 spokes, representing the 12 months.

Surya is also one of the Vedic pantheon's three supreme deities, along with Agni and Vayu, the wind god. Surya's family is quite prominent, with Surya regarded as the son of Dyaus Pita and Prithvi; Surya's wife is Sanjana, the daughter of Vishwakarma; Shani is one of Surya's sons. Vishwakarma, the celestial architect, sliced off some of Surya's dazzling light in the Puranas. This was done to diminish Surya's glow and make it easier for his daughter to withstand him. Furthermore, Vishwakarma has also created many other famous Hindu mythological weapons from Surya's blazing pieces, such as Vishnu's Shudarshana Chakra, Shiva's Trishul or trident, and Indra's Vajra.

The Rigveda mentions that Surya is at the center of the solar system. He is the leader of all the heavenly bodies. Surya exists in all of the universe's matter and elements. All planetary gods are collectively called navagraha, meaning nine celestial bodies. When creating a horoscope after a child's birth, these planets and heavenly bodies play a crucial role in astrology. The sun is the most important element in astrology, and its position impacts all the other celestial bodies.

In the Mahabharata, Kunti, the mother of the Pandavas, was one of the most prominent figures. Durvasa, a powerful sage, gave Kunti a boon that allowed her to chant a mantra and bear a child, one with divine qualities, by any god of her choosing. The young and unmarried princess wanted to test the mantra and so she invoked Surya, who blessed her with a son. However, as Kunti was an unwed woman at the time, concerned about the social stigma, she felt compelled to abandon her newborn son. The child was subsequently raised by a charioteer named Adhiratha Nandana and his wife, Radha, who named him Radheya. Later, this boy, with his radiant earrings and armor, came to be known as Karna. He grew into an exceptional warrior and was celebrated for his generous deeds. Though born out of wedlock and never given the status that was bestowed upon his Pandava brothers, he is one of the most notable, if not tragic, characters of the Mahabharata.

Surya is the god of excellence, glory and fame. Even the symbol of Surya is considered an auspicious sign. It is a symbol of victory in Hinduism. People have worshiped him at length, since eons, to receive his blessings. Surya Namaskar or sun salutation and offering water to the sun are the most direct ways of worshiping Surya. Thousands of Hindu devotees chant various mantras every day to praise him. The most famous and highly revered *Gayatri Mantra*, also known as the *Savitri Mantra*, from the Rigveda is associated with him. It calls upon Surya, the world's energy resource, for self-vitalization.

| ॐ भूर्भुवः स्वः तत्सवितुर्वरेण्यं |
॥ भर्गो देवस्य धीमहि धियो यो नः प्रचोदयात् ॥

Om Bhur-Bhuvah Svah Tat-Savitur-Varenyam,
Bhargo Devasya Dhimahi Dhiyo Yo Nah Prachodayat.

Translation

O Almighty God, you are the ultimate source
of knowledge and light, the destroyer of fear and
the creator of the universe. We humbly bow and
meditate upon your divine light, seeking guidance
and direction for our intellect.

—*Rigveda (Chapter 3, Verse 62)*

Furthermore, the legendary Syamantaka mani or jewel, features as a fascinating tale in the Vishnu Purana and the Bhagavata Purana. This mystical gemstone, originally worn by Surya around his neck, was renowned for its extraordinary properties of bringing prosperity and protection from misfortune to its keeper. One of the jewel's most captivating attributes was its ability to generate immense wealth daily for its owner. The jewel was later entrusted to Satrajit, a devoted follower of Surya, who became its custodian.

In certain regions of India, Surya is worshiped as Surya Narayana, signifying reverence for both Vishnu and Surya himself. In other parts, Surya is regarded as Ashtamurti or one of the eight aspects of Shiva. Surya has numerous temples across India and abroad, with the most renowned being the Sun Temple in Konark, Odisha, celebrated for its architectural grandeur and religious significance.

Several major Hindu festivals honor Surya, including Makar Sankranti, Pongal, Samba Dashami, Ratha Sapthami, Chath Puja and Kumbh Mela, highlighting Surya's importance in Hindu religious practices and cultural traditions.

LORD AGNI
The God of Fire

Agni holds a significant position in the Vedas. The Rigveda features over 200 hymns that praise Agni, highlighting his immense power and importance in the Vedic pantheon. There is no major ceremony in Hinduism that is complete without inviting Agni for the yagna's offering. The yagna is one of the oldest rituals in Hinduism. It is mentioned more than 1,184 times in the Vedas, of which 580 times is in the Rigveda.

|| यज्ञो वै श्रेष्ठं कर्मः ||

Yagyo Vai Shreshtham Karmah.

Translation
Yagna is the best karma.

—*Shatpath Brahman*

Yagna is a means to establish a connection with one's inner self and the soul in order to achieve peace of mind. This ritual has been practiced since the pre-Vedic period. It is assumed that any offering made with gratitude and belief reaches God through the fire during a yagna. Agni is blended with the yagna, the sacrificial fire that is supposed to carry the offerings made by individuals to God, like a messenger. Different terms are used for yagna like havana, hotrah, yajnah and agnihotra.

The Vedas mention more than 400 types of yagnas. Almost all Vedic scholars divided the Vedas into two parts: the Karmakanda, which consists of the action or sacrificial ritual-related sections, and the Jnanakanda, which issues the philosophy of life. The process of a yagna is also considered the most crucial karma in the Karmakanda of the Vedas. There are various reasons to perform yagnas, including the worship of Vedic gods.

Agni was born along with water. Therefore, he is a brother to Varuna, the god of water. Agni is often portrayed as a ruddy, two-faced god; the two faces represent two types of fire: immortality and life. Clad in a yellow silk cloth, he has three to seven tongues, three legs, seven arms and hair that stands on ends like flames. He rides a male sheep, the usual sacrificial animal. Further, Agni's three legs represent the three sacred fires—marriage, the nuptial fire; yagna, the ceremonial fire; and the funeral fire. It is believed that Agni does not discriminate among his believers and visits everyone, irrespective of their caste or creed, whether they are rich or poor. He holds the knowledge of the origins of the devas and humans, thus connecting them. The very first shloka in the Rigveda is devoted to Agni:

| अग्निमीळे पुरोहितं। यज्ञस्य देवमृ त्विजम्।
होतारं रत्नधातमम्॥

Agnimeele purohitam. Yagyasya devamritwijam.
Hotaram ratnadhaatmam.

Translation

I meditate on Agni, the priest of the sacrifice,
the divine immortal one who is essential to the
ritual, and the one who bestows wealth.
Let us not underestimate the power of Agni
and embrace his transformative force, as a mediator
between humans and the divine, emphasizing his
significance in bringing prosperity and blessings.

—*Rigveda (1.1.1)*

There are many fascinating stories about Agni in the Upanishads and other epics. One popular tale recounts how Agni offended the great seer Bhrigu, who then cursed him. The curse ensured that anything Agni touched would be destroyed. Frightened by the curse, Agni sought forgiveness from Brahma. Although Brahma couldn't lift the curse, he altered it so that Agni's touch would also purify whatever he touched and assured him that offerings to the gods would be delivered through Agni.

Another incident, from the Ramayana, tells us that Sita was asked to conduct Agni Pariksha or a trial by fire. Agni was the witness when Sita proved her innocence to Rama. He confirmed that Sita was chaste, and condemned Rama and the entire community for her tribulations. It is beyond anyone's individual ability to estimate the infinite strength of Agni.

All the varied forms of fire we find on Earth are parts of Agni. Of all the devas, Agni is closest to the living beings. In fact, Agni is a protector of all human beings and has a place in every home. He is the great god and messenger of the devas, worshiped by our ancestors. Agni, like Indra and Surya, was a major god during the Vedic period. Agni is eternally significant for people. Life on Earth cannot thrive without the blessings of the god of fire. In the Vedas, Agni is also mentioned as Brahman, the purest.

Even in modern Hinduism, Agni is an integral part of various traditions. Yagnas are sacred Hindu rituals that have been passed down through generations. Today, yagnas and rituals are performed to achieve peace, satisfaction, good health, cleanse sinful karma and improve relationships. In some parts of India, yagnas and rituals are performed for good rain, smooth crop harvesting, to invoke ancestors, ward off evil spirits and prevent natural disasters. Sometimes, it is performed to overcome obstacles and difficulties in life. Yagnas are conducted to achieve goals like dharma, artha and moksha. To perform yagnas, Agni must be present. Hinduism teaches that everything in the universe, including humans, plants, animals, mountains and fire, comprises the five elements. Fire is one of these elements, and it plays a crucial role in yagna offerings. Without Agni, no sacred yagna can be completed.

LORD YAMA
The God of Death

Yama is a highly revered figure in Hinduism, also known as the god of death and dharma. He rules over Yamloka, where souls are judged based on their actions during their time on Earth. By his side is Chitragupta, who meticulously records all of an individual's deeds to determine whether the soul will go to Svarga or face penance in Naraka or Hell. His record of everyone's good or bad deeds are in a register called Agrasandhani.

After death, souls reach Yama's palace. His guards are known as Vaidhyata and Kalapurusa. They guard the Yamloka. A person's good and evil deeds are read out in Yama's court by Chitragupta from the Agrasandhani. The soul is given a sentence that reflects the actions of the person during their life. If the person's soul is good and they have committed good deeds, then as per karma, they are sent to Svarga; otherwise, they are sent to one of the 21 levels of Naraka— where the lower levels have the worst punishment—or even back to Earth, in another form, to live another life. According to ancient stories, Yama is believed to be the eldest and the first mortal child of Surya. His sister, Yami, is associated with the Yamuna River, symbolizing the flow and continuity of life. In art, Yama is often depicted riding a powerful water buffalo whose strength represents his authority and the idea of justice and punishment. He carries a staff, symbolizing his role in ensuring that justice is served. Hemamala, Yama's wife, is specifically associated with the funeral pyre and is regarded as a goddess who oversees the rituals for the deceased, guiding them to the afterlife. While Yama is sometimes mentioned to have other wives, such as Vijaya and Susila, Hemamala's role is more prominent in certain traditions. She embodies the connection between the living and the departed, ensuring that the rites are performed correctly for a safe passage to the next world.

Yama's presence is felt throughout all Hindu scriptures like the Vedas, Upanishads, Puranas and the epic tales. He is seen as the eternal guide for souls, ensuring that they find their rightful place in the grand scheme of existence. Beyond judgment, Yama embodies compassion and wisdom about life's transitions. In Hindu cosmology, death isn't seen as an end but as a crucial step in the continuous cycle of rebirth and spiritual growth.

The fate of evil and the punishments meted out for various immoral deeds are mentioned in the Puranas. And it should be noted that Yama is also known as the "king of many hells." In the Vishnu Purana, we can find details of many dreadful hells, that are Yama's provinces, terrible tortures and fiery tools. In the Rigveda, only one dark hell is mentioned, but it does not appear as a place of torture. In the Brahmanas, hell is mentioned as a singular place of suffering. Whereas, in the Manusmriti, there are 21 types of suffering; the Agni Purana mentions only 4 hells, although some texts argue the number is 7; the Bhagavata Purana, the Vishnu Purana and the Devi Bhagavata Purana enlist and describe 28 hells.

Tamisra is a place of darkness where the sinful are punished by the Yamadutas and they perish without food or water. Andhatamisra is another hell where sinister beings are tortured, beaten up with sticks and scalded until they lose consciousness. Shukaramukha, meaning "hog's mouth," is a hell where the corrupt are crushed like sugarcane, and the sinful spirit is punished until it grieves and faints. There are many more hells, like Kumbhipakam where sinners are cooked in a pot. Actions such as theft lead souls to Tamisra, while those involved in crimes like cow slaughter or murder may face punishment in Rodh Naraka. Selling meat is believed to condemn one to Puyavaha Naraka. These hells represent different forms of suffering and purification, reflecting the complex moral framework of Hindu cosmology.

Yama is an important god in the Vedas. He frequently appears in the Puranas, the Manusmriti, the Ramayana and the Mahabharata. In an ancient tale about Yama, it is mentioned that he was originally handsome and charming, which made him popular among women. However, his popularity led to distractions, causing him to shirk some of his duties. This led to a rise in evil deeds in the world, as people no longer feared death. In response, Shiva cursed Yama, causing him to lose his attractive appearance and transform into an ugly form. As a result, Yama's complexion turned blue, and he began wearing red clothes while riding a water buffalo. This transformation underscored Yama's role as a stern and formidable deity, emphasizing the importance of his responsibilities in maintaining cosmic order and justice. Yama's complexion is described differently in various scriptures—sometimes red, sometimes blue—reflecting his dual nature: fearsome, yet necessary for maintaining the cosmic balance.

In contemporary India, Yama is honored on special occasions such as Naraka Chaturdashi and Yama Tharpanam.

Some temples, like the Dharmeswar Temple, are dedicated specifically to him. In many temples of Shiva, idols of Yama and Chitragupta can also be found. Yama holds significance as one of the rulers of the eight directions, particularly as the ruler of the southern region, and is revered during Ashtadikpalakas Pooja. He is known by various names, including Dharmaraja, which signifies his role as a judge, as well as Yamaraj, Dharma, Pitripeti, Mritu or Kaal. These aspects highlight his importance in Hindu cosmology and religious practices.

LORD VISHWAKARMA
The Divine Celestial Architect

Vishwakarma is another prominent deity in the Vedas. He is revered as the divine craftsman, architect and engineer. Known as the architect of the universe, he is also the official creator of palaces, heavenly abodes, royal residences, weapons and the mounts of gods. His name appears in the tenth book of the Rigveda, where Vishwakarma translates to "all maker," as "vishwa" means "all" and "karma" refers to "doer."

Depicted with four hands, Vishwakarma wears a crown and gold adornments. His hands hold a waterpot, a book, a noose and various tools of craftsmanship. According to Vedic texts, Vishwakarma had five sons, who inherited his skills, and two daughters—Sanjana, who wed Surya, and Saranya, who married Vaivasvata Manu. This portrayal underscores

Vishwakarma's pivotal role as a divine artisan, and the lineage of skilled craftsmanship that he passed down through his descendants in Hindu mythology.

In Hinduism, Vishwakarma is known as the god who sees everything. He is the one who created Heaven and Earth, knows all the worlds and grants the gods their names. In Puranic times, he was referred to as shilpkar or a mere craftsman. He is shown as the god of carpenters, goldsmiths, blacksmiths, masons and other artisans. Several scriptures describe him as the designer of flying chariots and divine weapons. Vishwakarma created numerous weapons and warships, including the Vajra for Indra, Sudarshana Chakra for Vishnu, the Trishul made from sun dust for Shiva, Pushpaka Vimana and many more.

According to a tale, Dadhichi, a rishi, was one of the most prominent devotees of Shiva. Once, he visited Mount Kailash as the teacher of Sati (an incarnation of Parvati). Shiva was pleased with the sage's devotion. He blessed Dadhichi with a boon that transformed his bones into thunder and provided him with the *Mahamrityunjaya Mantra*, thereby immortalizing him. At the same time, there happened to be an asura called Vritra. He had received a boon that protected him from weapons made up of metal, iron, wood and fire. All the gods, including Indra, prayed to Vishnu to defeat the demon. Vishnu told Indra that the only way to kill Vritra was with the bones of the powerful Dadhichi. Indra was, however, afraid of approaching Dadhichi for this sacrifice. But when the sage learned about this, he immediately consented to lay down his life for the gods. However, no one could create weapons from the bones of Dadhichi. Ultimately, it was Vishwakarma who came forward to craft a weapon that helped Indra defeat the demon.

Vishwakarma built most of the well-known palaces mentioned in Hindu scriptures. The Svarga of Indra is one of his masterpieces. His other wonder is the Golden City of Lanka, a mansion built for Shiva and Parvati, although they could not live there. According to the Puranas, Ravana was invited to perform the Grihapravesh ritual at Shiva and Parvati's abode. It was a golden palace, and Ravana was awestruck by its beauty. Shiva told Ravana to ask for anything as his dakshina or offering. Mesmerized by the palace's elegance and grandeur, Ravana asked for the palace itself. Among the many mythical towns, Vishwakarma built Dwarka, the capital of Krishna's city, and the Maya Sabha of the Pandavas.

Since Vishwakarma is the divine designer of the universe, the engineering and architectural communities revere him. It is customary for artisans to worship their tools in his name. Even today, Vishwakarma Jayanti is celebrated on Kanya Sankranti of the Hindu calendar. This festival is predominantly observed in factories, industrial areas, shops, etc. It is a day of worship for artisans, craftsmen, mechanics, smiths, industrial workers and factory workers. They gather to pray for lasting prosperity, safe working conditions and personal achievements.

In Hindu tradition, workers across various professions hold their tools in high regard, seeing them as instrumental to their livelihoods and financial success. For instance, barbers venerate their scissors, farmers honor plows and cultivators, students revere their books, clerks worship pens, potters respect their wheels, blacksmiths hold their hammers in reverence and soldiers worship their guns and weapons. This practice has persisted for millennia, highlighting the deep cultural significance of tools and craftsmanship in Hindu society.

LORD CHANDRA
The Moon God

Chandra, the moon god, is a lunar deity and an important Vedic god. Chandra means moon in Sanskrit. As per Hindu astrology, it is also one of the nine heavenly bodies that influence life on Earth. About 114 hymns are dedicated to Chandra in the ninth mandala of the Rigveda. Chandra is a young, intelligent, four-armed god. He has a weapon in one hand and a lotus in the other. He rides a chariot pulled by 10 white horses and flies across the sky during the night.

In Hinduism, Chandra is a complex deity to understand because of the various interpretations found in different scriptures. He is believed to have power over the mind and can activate speech, and, consequently, is called Vachaspati, the god of speech. He is also known as the god of plants and vegetation, which is why Chandra and Soma are two names often used interchangeably for the same god. In some Puranic texts, soma is an intoxicating drink for the immortal gods and drinking it makes one immortal. It is made from a magical plant with white flowers. This sacred plant is a small creeper without leaves. It creates an exceptional liquid substance—nectar—that can remove all obstacles for any person, god or demon in this universe.

There are several stories in the Hindu scriptures that are linked to Chandra. In an interesting tale from the Vedic period, Chandra fell in love with Tara, the wife of Brihaspati, the planet Jupiter. Chandra was captivated by her beauty and elegance, and Tara, too, was attracted to him. Chandra managed to abduct her and make her his queen. The two of them even had a child—Buddh, the planet Mercury. However, because Brihaspati was a powerful deity, he declared war on Chandra, which caused chaos among all the deities of the Vedic period. Soon, all the devas went to Brahma and requested that he intervene. After a long debate, it was decided that Tara would go back to Brihaspati and Chandra was asked to apologize for his actions. When his love was sent back to Brihaspati, Chandra was left distraught.

Later, he married Daksha's 27 daughters. Among all his wives, Rohini was the one he favored the most. The other 26 became disconcerted as Chandra spent the most time with her. They complained to Daksha about it, who then cursed Chandra, making the moon god weak and faded. To lift the curse, he dedicated himself to Shiva and began to pray to him. Because of his devotion, Shiva partially lifted the curse. This came to be symbolized by the phase of the lunar eclipse when the moon appears to fade away but doesn't completely vanish; it reflects Chandra's enduring connection to Shiva and the cyclical nature of the moon's phases. Additionally, Chandra's wives—Rohini, Tara, Anuradha and Bharani—are among the 27 Nakshatras or constellations. Moreover, Chandra is a significant god for several reasons. Many universally practiced rituals are performed to please him. He oversees several important aspects of our lives, even bringing fortune and health.

Several prominent Hindu festivals are dedicated to Chandra. One such festival is Chandra Darshan, celebrated in Maharashtra, India, and is also observed in Nepal. In Vedic astrology, Chandra holds significant importance as one of the key heavenly bodies in a person's birth chart. Devotees often chant the *Chandra Mantra* to alleviate the effects of any adverse positions of the moon in their horoscopes.

Monday is traditionally associated with the moon, as it is governed by Chandra, making it an auspicious day for lunar worship. Therefore, it is understandable why in the Hindu calendar, Monday is known as Somavara, derived from the word "soma." In Hinduism and Hindu astrology, Chandra also symbolizes the mind, feminine qualities, beauty and happiness.

MINOR DEITIES OF
THE VEDIC PANTHEON

The Rigveda has thousands of hymns, mostly dedicated to specific deities and gods. Some dedications are to paired deities, such as Indra–Agni, Mitra–Varuna and Soma–Rudra. Some hymns are dedicated to the Vishvedevas who are invoked more than 70 times in the text. Although many other deities are mentioned in the Vedas, some have less than 20–30 hymns inscribed to them. Many are only addressed by one or two hymns. All such gods are categorized as minor deities of the Vedic pantheon. A few of them are Vastospati, Ushas, Savitr, Maruts, Pushan, Dyaus, Rudra, Mitra, Vayu, Apas, Brahmanaspati, Manyu, Nirrti, Manas, Dakshina, Purusha, Bhaga, Vasukra, Atri, Apam Napat, Ksetrapati, Ghrta, Asamati, Urvasi, Pururavas, Vena, Aranyani, Mayabheda, Tarksya, Tvashtar and Saranyu.

Many of these deities rose to prominence in the Puranic period. Some had tales in the Puranas or occupied a secondary role. The following are some of the minor Vedic gods that we have been able to identify:

Rudra: Rudra, a minor Vedic deity, is one of the names of Shiva. Considered to be a major god in modern Hinduism, his presence in the Vedic scriptures, however, is much less prominent. In these texts, he is associated with storms, winds, hunting and healing, and is more often feared than loved. Rudra is described as severe, fierce and unpredictable, earning the title "mightiest of the mighty" in the Yajurveda. He is depicted as the divine archer who shoots arrows of death and disease.

Rudra is also considered the ancestor of the Rudras, the hurricane gods, also known as the Maruts, who are associated with storms and climate. According to some scholars, initially, the associations with Shiva are scant in the Vedic texts, with most references only mentioning Rudra as a fierce and stormy deity. However, by the end of the Rigvedic period, Rudra gained more prominence. In the Puranic period, Rudra finally evolved into Shiva, one of the principal deities of Hinduism. This transformation reflects the syncretic nature of Hinduism, where earlier Vedic deities often merged with or transformed into the later Puranic gods. Additionally, the Mahamrityunjaya Mantra, one of the most famous mantras dedicated to Rudra, is found in both the Rigveda and the Yajurveda. This mantra (a few lines of which are given below) further seeks to indicate the connection between Rudra and Shiva, with the latter evolving from the figure of Rudra over time, embodying both his fierce and compassionate aspects. Worshiping Rudra is recommended for those seeking moksha or liberation.

॥ ॐ त्र्यम्बकं यजामहे सुगन्धिं पुष्टिवर्धनम् उर्वारुकमिव बन्धनान् मृत्योर्मुक्षीय माऽमृतात् ॥

Aum, Trayambakam Yajaamahe sugandhim pushtivardhanam,
urvarukamiva bandhanaan mrityormuksheeya maamritaat.

Translation

We worship the three-eyed one [Shiva],
who is fragrant and nourishes all beings.
May he liberate us from the bondage
of worldly attachments and death, and grant
us immortality [i.e., when death comes].

—*Rigveda (7.59.12)*

It is in the Shvetashvatara Upanishad, that Rudra is called Shiva for the first time, and is depicted as the creator, preserver and destroyer of all creation. In the Rigveda, three entire hymns are devoted to Rudra. Additionally, he is mentioned about 75 times.

Varuna: Varuna is revered as the king of the universe and the sky. As one of the oldest and most significant Vedic deities, he is prominently mentioned in many hymns of the Rigveda. Varuna means "he who covers," signifying his all-pervasive presence over the entire world. In the Vedas, Varuna is associated with the sky, but in the Puranas, his domain extends to the oceans, making him the god of the oceans. Varuna is also connected to clouds, water and rivers, and is considered the father of the Vedic seer Vashishta.

In the Vedas, Varuna is described as having 1,000 eyes, enabling him to oversee the world. Initially, he is called the king of the universe in Vedic hymns, but later, he loses his supreme authority to Indra and other Puranic gods. Varuna is often depicted riding on a crocodile, holding a lotus, noose, conch and a vessel of gems. An umbrella formed by the hood of a cobra, named Abhoga, is also held over his head.

In contemporary rituals, worshiping Varuna remains an essential practice. He is still revered as the Guardian of the West in some regions, underscoring his enduring significance in Hindu traditions.

In one of the tales of the Ramayana, Rama sought the permission of Varuna to cross the ocean, so that he and his army could reach Lanka. For three consecutive days and nights, Rama prayed to Varuna but received no response. On the fourth day, frustrated and angry, Rama prepared to attack the ocean and loaded an arrow on his bow. Seeing this, Varuna finally emerged from the ocean. Bowing to Rama, Varuna explained that he was at a loss on how to assist him as the sea was deep and vast, and could not change its nature. He also reminded Rama, "You are the soul of peace and love; wrath does not suit you."

Varuna then promised Rama that he would not disturb his army. With Varuna's assurance, Rama and his forces could build a bridge and go over to Lanka. Upon crossing the ocean, Rama led his army to Lanka, where a fierce battle ensued. Ultimately, Varuna's gesture contributed to Rama triumphing over the demon king Ravana, rescuing his wife, Sita, and restoring dharma. This tale underscores the themes of perseverance, righteousness and the ultimate victory of good over evil.

Prithvi: In the Rigveda, the goddess of Earth is the mother of Indra and Agni, and the consort of Dyaus Pita. She is also known as Bhumi or Bhudevi. Other epithets include Dhara, Dharti and Dharitri—names that mean "she who holds everything." Prithvi and Dyaus are also symbolized as cows and bulls in many scriptures.

Prithvi and Dyaus, the early deities of the Vedas, were also worshiped as fertility gods and they engendered all the other gods. Prithvi is depicted with four arms, holding Komud, a blue lotus; a water vessel; a bowl of healing herbs; and another bowl containg vegetables. At times, one of her left hands is shown depicting the fearless Abhaya Mudra as well. She is depicted as riding on the backs of four elephants, which represent the four corners of the world. In the Puranas, Prithvi is an avatar of Lakshmi.

According to the Ramayana, Sita is the daughter of Bhumi. She was discovered in a trench in a cultivated field by Janaka of Mithila. Later, at the end of her life, she returned to her mother, the earth's womb. In the Rigveda, Prithvi is never alone. She is always next to Dyaus, the male deity associated with the sky. By and large, in the Vedas, Dyaus and Prithvi are the parents of the other gods. Further, the Atharvaveda has many hymns dedicated to Prithvi.

Several other minor Vedic gods also played significant roles in the early Vedic religion. For example:

Aryaman: A god associated with maintaining the social order and societal relationships, Aryaman is often invoked in the context of marriage and hospitality.

Bhaga: A god of wealth and prosperity, Bhaga is invoked for blessings of abundance and good fortune. He is one of the Adityas, a group of solar deities.

Tvashtar: A form of Vishwakarma, Tvashtar is a divine artisan and craftsman, and is the maker of divine implements. He is sometimes considered to be the forger of the thunderbolt used by Indra.

Ushas or Usas: The goddess of dawn, who brings light and chases away the darkness, Ushas is celebrated for her beauty and vitality, symbolizing renewal and hope.

Though not as prominently worshiped as the major Vedic gods, these minor gods contribute to the rich tapestry of the Vedic period. Their roles and attributes reflect upon the various aspects of nature, society and the cosmos.

THE PURANIC
GODS

Hinduism is remarkably capable of adapting and integrating with the new, while preserving its traditional foundations. This has resulted in a diverse religious environment where ancient gods are revered alongside contemporary spiritual leaders and movements. The emphasis on universal values, such as compassion, caring for nature, spirituality and selfless service, has enabled Hinduism to remain relevant and attractive to both long-standing devotees and newer generations.

Present-day Hinduism is divided into various devotional sects and denominations, each with its own beliefs, philosophies and communities. The Rigveda contains a well-known adage in Book 1, Verse 46, "Ekam sat vipra bahudha vadanti," which translates to "Truth is one, sages call it by different names."

Therefore, despite the hundreds of deities and various different practices surrounding the religion, Hindus worship a single Supreme God—an ultimate reality that can be comprehended and expressed in diverse ways by each sect.

The three sampradayas or commonly recognized traditions are Vaishnavism, Shaivism and Shaktism. These traditions are centered around Vishnu, Shiva and Shakti, respectively. Other gods such as Brahma, Hanuman, Ganesha, etc., are also considered essential in Hinduism. All these traditions follow nearly identical rituals, practices and worship methods. The gods previously mentioned are predominant Puranic divinities, and their stories, attributes and worship practices are elaborated in the Puranas, the Ramayana, the Mahabharata and other scriptures. These scriptures constitute a genre of post-Vedic literature from the Indian subcontinent, encompassing historical, spiritual and religious teachings.

Vaishnavism is a sect in which Vishnu is considered the supreme and his avatars are worshiped too. It is the largest Hindu denomination, making up 60–70 percent of the religion's devotee composition. The two most prominently worshiped avatars are Rama and Krishna from the Ramayana and the Mahabharata, respectively. Vaishnavism includes several subsects, one of which is Sri Vaishnavism. This subsect is based on the teachings of Ramanujacharya, a revered guru, philosopher and one of the most significant proponents of the tradition. Another subsect is Sadh Vaishnavism, which emphasizes devotion to Vishnu and his incarnations, particularly Krishna and Rama. In contrast, Advaita Vedanta presents a different philosophical perspective. It teaches that everything in the universe is ultimately one, asserting that the individual soul (atman) is identical to the universal soul (Brahman). While each wave in the ocean may be a separate entity, they all originate from the same water. Similarly, as per Advaita Vedanta, each individual soul is unique but ultimately part of the same divine essence.

Parallelly, Shaivism worships Shiva as the Supreme God. In this sect, avatars are not observed. Shiva is recognized as neither male nor female, as the god is believed to be beyond the constraints of any gender. There are many subsects or schools of Shaivism, like Shaiva Siddhanta, Shiva Advaita and Aghori.

On the other hand, Shaktism believes in and worships Devi or the Divine Mother. Shakti has many forms, like Durga, Kali and Parvati. In this sect, the Divine Mother is worshiped as the highest god. The divine Devi is honored in different forms; some are fierce, whereas others are soft and gentle. Shaktism also includes practices such as yoga, rituals with sacred diagrams (yantras), the awakening of Kundalini energy and the exploration of mystical abilities.

In addition, there is another sect called Smartas, who believe that the Puranic gods—Brahma, Vishnu and Shiva— are equal, as they were created by Brahman, the one Supreme God (not to be confused with Brahma).

In the present day, the major practices of Hinduism are largely influenced by key ancient texts, specifically the Puranas, the Ramayana, the Mahabharata and the Bhagavad Gita. Furthermore, we can say, post-Vedic literature is the encyclopedia of present-day Hinduism. It consists of abstract philosophy, information about festivals, temples, rituals, astronomy and genealogies of gods, goddesses, kings, heroes, ancient sages and demigods. The epics, Ramayana and Mahabharata, form the Itihasas, which are believed to be composed in the later epochs, the period of the Puranas, the post-Vedic age. In Hinduism, these epics have a significant role to play. If someone wants to understand Hinduism, they should read the epics to grasp the religion's core values. These epics influence present-day art, culture, attire, family, relationships, literature, festivals, plays and movies.

***

The Puranas: The Puranic scriptures are very different from the Vedas. Purana is a Sanskrit word that means "old or ancient." There are no references to the Ramayana, Mahabharata or the Puranas in the Vedas. But the Puranas make revelations about the Vedas. In the latter, multiple significant deities were worshiped, and the scriptures were standardized for everyone. Several versions of the same Puranas can be found in various parts of India. In the Puranas, a single God is extolled; a particular Purana is dedicated to this one God. The Puranas contain epic poems, verses and stories that explain Hinduism and emphasize the importance of religious rituals, duties, and the evolution of practices, beliefs and philosophies over time. These enormous texts are the work of ancient rishis. Veda Vyasa, the narrator of the Mahabharata, who classified the Vedas, is widely credited with compiling the Puranas too. The 18 Mukhya or Mahapuranas are the primary texts, and the 18 Upapuranas are considered secondary in authority. Together, they contain more than 400,000 verses.

Below is the list of 18 Mahapuranas:

Brahma Purana	Brahmanda Purana
Padma Purana	Linga Purana
Vishnu Purana	Varaha Purana
Shiva Purana	Skanda Purana
Bhagavata Purana	Vamana Purana
Narada Purana	Kurma Purana
Markandeya Purana	Matsya Purana
Agni Purana	Garuda Purana
Bhavishya Purana	Brahmavaivarta Purana

There are a few variations in the authorities of those included in the list of Mahapuranas. The Kurma Purana's list substitutes the Vayu Purana for the Agni Purana as one of the Mahapuranas. Similarly, the Agni Purana omits the Shiva Purana and introduces the Vayu Purana. The Brahma Purana substitutes the Garuda Purana with the Upapurana called the Narashima Purana. Even though, the Puranas are specific to a deity, the texts are sometimes mixed and revere multiple gods and goddesses.

Roughly, the Puranas are classified as:

- The Puranas devoted to praising Brahma: Brahma Purana and Padma Purana.
- The Puranas that are related to Vishnu: Vishnu Purana, Bhagavata Purana, Naradeya Purana, Garuda Purana, Vayu Purana, Varaha Purana, Matsya Purana and Bhavishya Purana.
- The Puranas chiefly connected with Shiva: Shiva Purana, Varaha Purana, Linga Purana, Skanda Purana, Vamana Purana, Kurma Purana, Markandeya Purana and Brahmanda Purana.
- The Puranas based on Agni and Surya: Brahma Vaivarta Purana and Agni Purana

One of the most widely read and circulated Puranas is the Vishnu Purana. It touches on the universe's creation, Brahman's destruction and re-creation, the genealogy of gods and goddesses, the period and reign of Manu and much more. The Puranas were composed primarily in Sanskrit but have been translated into Tamil and other Indian languages as well. The Bhagavata Purana is also popular, as it is held in the highest esteem by Vaishnavas across all parts of India.

The Upapuranas refer to the category of Hindu religious texts that are considered secondary to the Mahapuranas. Upapuranas are typically shorter and less extensive in scope. They provide additional insights into specific aspects of cosmogony, mythology, genealogy and other traditional religious teachings of Hindu religious literature. However, there are some variations about the number of Upapuranas. The Matsya Purana says only four Upapuranas exist, but the Devi Bhagavata Purana enumerates 18.

Below is the list of 18 Upapuranas:

Adya Purana (Sanatkumara)	Parasara Purana
Narasimha Purana	Samba Purana
Skanda Purana	Kalika Purana
Shivadharma Purana	Nandi Purana
Durvasa Purana	Vasishtha Purana
Naradiya Purana	Mudgala Purana
Kapila Purana	Sanat-kumara Purana
Vamana Purana	Ekamra Purana
Aushanasa Purana	Kalika Purana

Several Upapuranas,* including the Adi Purana, Ganesh Purana, etc., may not be included on the list due to variations in regional interpretations, scriptural differences and different scholarly interpretations.

***

In addition to the Vedas and Puranas, there are other important scriptures in Hinduism as well. The two great epics—the Ramayana and the Mahabharata—are important to the religion. They highlight the significance of history in present-day Hinduism, which revolves around epics and gods. The Ramayana and Mahabharata emphasize on the righteous path, which is described as dharma. However, the word "dharma" does not appear to be a dominant concept in the Vedic period. Irrespective of that, the dharma narratives were central to Hinduism in the two epics. The influence of dharma on Hinduism changed the concept's focus to duty. Both epics feature very similar ideologies, stories and ideas. They represent Hindu mythology and culture in rich detail, and have entirely assimilated the religion.

The Ramayana: The Ramayana is the ideal guidebook for the various relationships in one's life. It has influenced nearly all of Southeast Asia and every living being in India, as it describes the importance of staying on the road of dharma. It

---

* The total number of Puranas in Hinduism varies depending on different classifications and traditions. Generally, there are 18 Mahapuranas and an equal number of Upapuranas, making a total of 36 recognized texts in these categories. However, there are additional texts and variations in different lists, depending on regional and sectarian beliefs.

is Rama's tale, one of Vishnu's avatars, and the main focus of worship. Rama's journey through life is about how he responds to the difficulties that come his way. Known as Purushottam, representing the morally upright way, he is the epitome of the ideal human being. Hindu obligations, rights and societal responsibilities are metaphorically explained through the lives of Rama, Sita and their companions. The words "Rama" and "Ayana" make up the name Ramayana and refer to Rama's adventures. Guided by Brahma's instructions, Valmiki set out to compose the epic Ramayana. Ramayana has become a timeless tale. It teaches important lessons about doing what is right, fulfilling one's responsibilities, and underscores the ability to overcome mistakes and find redemption; Valmiki's text aims to inspire generations, teaching the values of righteousness, duty and the power of forgiveness.

The Valmiki Ramayana is divided into more than 500 chapters and is written in 7 kandas or books. It has more than 50,000 lines or 24,000 verses. The main characters are Rama, Sita and Ravana—the rakshasa who performed penance in the name of Shiva. Ravana was well renowned for practicing asceticism and meditation; he was a devotee of the god. Another important character is Lakshmana, the younger brother of Rama. Lakshmana's wife was Urmila, the younger sister of Sita, Rama's wife. Urmila was the lawful daughter of King Janaka of Mithila and Queen Sunayana, whereas Sita was her adoptive sister. Hanuman plays a critical role as Sugriva's advisor and a great devotee of Rama. In addition to these, there are numerous other characters, such as King Dasharatha, Vishwamitra, Ganga, Lav-Kush, Kaikeyi, Shatrughna, Maricha, Surpanakha, Sugriva, Angada, Vibhishana and Kumbhakarna.

The Mahabharata: The Mahabharata is another major epic written in Sanskrit. It is the story of a war fought for supremacy over the kingdom of Hastinapur.

It is estimated that more than 18 Akshauhinis (an Akshauhinis army consists of 109,350-foot soldiers, 21,870 chariots, 21,870 elephants and 65,610 horses) and approximately 47 lakh people participated in the war.[14]

The greatest battle in the history of Bharatvarsha was fought between the descendants of two brothers, Pandu and Dhritarashtra. Pandu had five sons: Yudhishthira, Bhima and Arjuna by his first wife, Kunti; and Nakula and Sahadeva by another wife, Madri. On the other hand, Dhritarashtra had a colossal family. He had 100 sons and 1 daughter, out of whom Duryodhana was the eldest. Being hateful, egoistic and sinister, he was exceedingly hostile toward his Pandu cousins. However, he was also a noble and trustworthy friend. The whole epic revolves around this family's quest for power and revenge. After the war, the Pandavas were victorious. But both sides suffered huge casualties. For the Pandavas, there were only eight survivors—the five Pandava brothers and Krishna, Satyaki and Yuyutsu. Whereas, for the Kauravas, the number was four—Ashwatthama; Kritavarma, the seer; Kripa; and Vrishaketu, the son of Karna.

The Mahabharata contains about 100,000 stanzas and approximately 1.8 million words, making it the longest epic poem in the world. It is organized into 18 books, known as Parvas. The author, Veda Vyasa, dictated the verses, while Ganesha wrote them down. With the ascension of the Pandava brothers to Svarga, the death of Krishna and the subsequent end of his dynasty, the Mahabharata comes to an end. It also marks the commencement of the Hindu age of

Kali Yuga, the fourth and final age according to Hinduism, where noble values and thoughts will crumble, and mankind will rapidly approach the resolution of progress, honesty and values.[15]

According to the concluding passage of this great epic, reading the Mahabharata destroys all sins. Furthermore, chanting mantras from the text purifies the mind and spirit, promoting inner peace and spiritual growth. It contains the history of gods and rishis. The epic poem also includes a record of the life and teachings of Krishna, the creator and ruler of the universe, one of the avatars of Vishnu.

The Bhagavad Gita: The Bhagavad Gita contains 700 verses. It is included in the Mahabharata (chapters 23–40 of Bhishma Parva). This Hindu scripture continues to be widely published, translated and read. The Bhagavad Gita narrates the conversations between Arjuna and his charioteer during the Kurukshetra war, Krishna. This scripture is said to help one escape the cycle of birth and death. Anyone who passionately reads the Bhagavad Gita will go to spiritual heaven after death. Reading the text is considered equivalent to studying all Vedic scriptures. One can go to the spiritual world by reciting even half a shloka.

The other parts of the vast, extensive and sacred literature of Hinduism include smritis, sutras and shastras. They are the effort of thousands of years of accumulated spiritual experience. However, they are not widely known and have not been extensively studied or researched.

LORD BRAHMA AND GODDESS SARASWATI

Brahma is one third of the chief Trinity of gods; he is part of the Brahma–Vishnu–Shiva Trimurti, the triplex deity of supreme divinity in Hinduism. The Trimurti symbolizes the Creation, the Maintenance and the Destruction of the universe. In this triad, Brahma is the creator god of Hinduism. He is also known as Svayambhu, the self-born god or the one who created himself. He is the father of many chief ancient sages, including the four Sanatkumaras: Manu, Narada Muni, Daksha and Marichi. Saraswati is Brahma's consort.

The birth of Brahma is described in the Rigveda through the concept of Hiranyagarbha or the golden cosmic egg. It tells of a time when there existed only an immense, eternal ocean stretching endlessly in every direction. Hiranyagarbha, a huge, shining golden egg, came out of this ocean. The egg, over time, cracked open and Brahma emerged from it. He had a wise, old look, and four heads with white beards. He sat gracefully on a large lotus flower that bloomed in the cosmic waters.

Once Brahma appeared, he began to create everything in the universe. He made the skies, the earth and all living things. From his imagination, he formed humans and wise seers who would understand the mysteries of life and creation.

His four heads, facing four different directions, are attributed to the creation of the four Vedas. In fact, each of his heads point toward a cardinal direction.

He is clothed in white or reddish-pink, with his vahana, Hansa, depicted as a swan or a goose, seated nearby. His hands symbolize knowledge and creation. They hold no weapon. In one hand, he holds the sacred texts of the Vedas. In the second, he holds a mala or rosary beads, symbolizing time. In the third, he holds a shankh or conch, or at times a ladle, that feeds the sacrificial fire. In the fourth, he has a kamandalu or a utensil with water, which conveys the emanation of all creation. However, different interpretations of these are mentioned in various scriptures.

Several versions of the Vishnu Purana describe Brahma as emerging from a lotus connected to Vishnu's navel. Similarly, various Shiva Puranas suggest that he was born from Shiva. Across diverse versions of Hindu mythology, Brahma is considered the Supreme God. However, in the present-day, Brahma does not enjoy popular worship. His consort, Saraswati, on the other hand is highly revered. There are various stories that talk about curses that have supposedly prevented Brahma from being worshiped on Earth.

According to one of them, it is because of Shiva's curse. Shiva Purana tells us that Brahma and Vishnu once argued about who was the most powerful amongst the Trimurti. When the argument got heated, Shiva intervened. He turned into a gigantic lingam, which was made of fire and light, and extended from Heaven to the underworld. Shiva told them that the one who was able to find the end of the light would be considered the most powerful. Brahma endeavored to trace the light's end but could not reach it. Nevertheless, not wanting to admit defeat, he began looking for a suitable witness who could vouch for his actions, even if it meant fabricating the truth—this is how he found a flower to testify before Shiva and lie to him, saying Brahma had indeed reached the uppermost part of the lingam and seen the end. The witness was the Ketaki flower that used to be placed at the topmost part of the lingam during worship. Shiva, however, found out about Brahma's deception, and cursed both him and the Ketaki flower. As a result, Brahma is not worshiped on Earth, and the Ketaki flower is no longer offered to Shiva. However, Vishnu expressed his respect for both deities and proposed that they all work together in maintaining balance in the universe. He urged Brahma to learn from this incident and to recognize that each god has a unique role in the cosmic cycle—Brahma as the creator, Vishnu as the preserver and Shiva as the destroyer.

Another tale is from the Padma Purana. It states that Brahma saw the asura Vajranabha trying to kill Brahma's sons and attack people. He then decided to conduct a yagna at the central Pushkar Lake. To accomplish his yagna without being attacked by demons, he created the hills around Pushkar. But his wife, Saraswati, could not be present at the allocated time to perform the necessary section of the yagna. Annoyed, Brahma found a milkman's daughter, who was virtuous and eligible to be his wife. Her name was Gayatri. She was known as the goddess of milk. Brahma then married Gayatri as he had to complete the yagna. When Saraswati finally arrived, she found Gayatri sitting next to Brahma. She became furious and cursed Brahma, ensuring that no one could worship him. Later Brahma apologized, and once her anger subsided, she reduced the curse and permitted his worship in Pushkar. Interestingly, based on Vastu Shastra, the Hindu science of architecture and design, a space for Brahma is reserved at the center of the base of the main sanctum in every Hindu temple.

A different version of the story states that the seer Bhrigu cursed Brahma when the creation god ignored his prayers. Bhrigu had invited Brahma to a significant yagna, but Brahma, being too immersed in the music that was being played by Saraswati, failed to pay any heed to the sage. Hence, Bhrigu got angry and denounced the god. These different stories about Brahma indicate why he is not as glorified as Shiva or Vishnu.

There are various names of Brahma: Abjaja, the one who is born from a lotus; Prajapati, the creation god; Vedanatha, Veda god; Gyaneshwara, god of knowledge; and Chaturmukha, the one with four faces. There are very few temples dedicated to him. The most famous being the Brahma Temple, in Pushkar, Rajasthan, and a shrine found in Angkor Wat in Cambodia. Furthermore, Brahma's name should not be confused with Brahman or Brahmin. Brahman refers to the Absolute or the Supreme Reality of Vedanta philosophy, whereas Brahmin refers to a person who belongs to the priestly class in the Hindu religion.

***

Saraswati, the esteemed consort of Brahma, holds a significant place in Hindu worship. Saraswati is the Hindu goddess of wisdom and knowledge. She is often depicted as a beautiful goddess, dressed in white, with a serene expression. Unlike other goddesses mostly portrayed as eager for matrimony and motherhood, Saraswati is aloof and detached. Her white complexion and attire signify her asceticism, transcendence and purity. She has four arms and is often depicted holding a veena, the Vedas and a kamandalu. At times, she is shown riding a swan or a peacock. There are specific Saraswati mantras to praise and worship the goddess. Many Hindus, especially children, students, scholars, intellectuals and musicians, worship Saraswati as the goddess of knowledge, music and learning. In festivals like Vasant Panchami, she is specifically worshiped by students, artists and scholars. While Brahma is the creator, Saraswati is seen as the force that brings order, creativity and understanding to his creations. This not only makes her integral to the creation process, but also revered prominently in Hindu culture as, education and learning hold significant importance in Hindu society.

Saraswati is also worshiped outside India. In Indonesia, particularly on the island of Bali, she is honored through ceremonies that celebrate knowledge and learning. Balinese Hindus observe a special "Saraswati Day" dedicated to her. In Japan, she is known as Benzaiten and is one of the Seven Lucky Gods. In Thai culture, Saraswati is called Surasawadee, and is recognized for her connection to education and the arts. Similarly, in Nepal, she is worshiped with great devotion, especially during the festival of Basant Panchami, much like in India. In Myanmar, she is revered as Thurathadi or Tipitaka Medaw. Saraswati is a member of the Tridevi, the trinity of goddess consorts for the gods of the Trimurti—Saraswati, Lakshmi and Parvati. They help to create and maintain the universe with Brahma, Vishnu and Shiva.

In a famous tale from the Brahma Purana, there was chaos and a lack of structure at the beginning of the world. There was noise but no music, speech, wisdom, art or inspiration. Brahma meditated deeply to address this disorder, and from his divine meditation emerged Saraswati, the goddess of wisdom, music, arts and learning. Her creation brought light to the dark and chaotic universe. Saraswati's first act was to play her veena, and as her fingers moved over the strings, she filled the cosmos with melodious music. The chaotic sounds turned into harmonious music, and the disorder of creation began to take on an orderly pattern. Her music inspired the sages and artists, endowing them with creativity and wisdom. The words of the Vedas were revealed to the sages, and knowledge spread across the world. Saraswati's arrival brought harmony and light to the universe. With her beautiful music, she laid the foundation for knowledge and creativity. This turned chaos into a lovely song of life, helping people find wisdom and inspiration in their art and learning.

LORD VISHNU AND GODDESS LAKSHMI

Vishnu is another part of the Hindu Trinity. A highly revered and notable deity, he is also the most worshiped god in Hinduism. He also serves as the preserver in the triad. Vishnu maintains the universe, which is periodically created by Brahma and regularly destroyed by Shiva, to prepare for the next cycle of Brahma's creation. He is revered as the greatest god in Vaishnavism, the most significant of the Hindu sects. He is identical to Brahman's metaphysical concept—the atman, the unchanging ultimate reality—like the one inside every living body or as the absolute or supreme. Vishnu was not a principal god like Indra or Agni in the Vedic period. However, in the Puranic period, he was promoted to being one of Hinduism's most important gods. The notion of avatar in Hinduism started with Vishnu and is most often associated with only him. The concept of an avatar is a god reincarnating as a human. The avatars are majorly found in the Puranas. Whenever any great disaster strikes the lives of good people and evil forces threaten to rule the world, Vishnu the preserver comes to Earth as an animal, human or semi-human to challange the darkness. Vishnu's avatars empower the good and destroy the evil, restore dharma and relieve Earth's burden. The list of Vishnu's avatars is elaborated in later sections of this book.

Some Puranas mention that Brahma was born from a lotus flower that grew from Vishnu's navel; this scene has been portrayed in many works of art, and the imagery associated with it continues to be quite popular, finding its way into today's mass media artwork. This symbolic representation of the cosmic equilibrium of finite within the infinite is called Sri Padmanabha in Anantashayan. Vishnu is also called Narayana, meaning "dweller and the guardian of human beings." He is married to Lakshmi, the goddess of wealth. The famous *Narayana Mantra* is chanted to please Vishnu.

|| ॐ नमो नारायणाय ||

Om Namo Narayanaya.

Translation

I bow before the Almighty.

—*Tarasara Upanishad*

Vishnu is mostly portrayed with skin that is blue in color, like the sky. But, at times, he is also depicted with a black complexion. The posture of this four-armed god can be standing or resting. He wears a necklace made of the famous Kaustubha gem and a five-row garland. He holds a shankha, a chakra, a gada and a padma or lotus. His lower right hand is in Abhaya Mudra, depicting fearlessness. Like any other god, Vishnu has a vahana, too. His vehicle is Garuda, a huge bird-like creature with a white face, red wings and an eagle's beak.

Vishnu is easily pleased with prayers. Hence, chanting the *Vishnu Mantra* brings good health, happiness and prosperity. He is revered as the remover of all obstacles and fear. In Hinduism, worshiping Vishnu with tulsi leaves or lotus flowers is considered highly beneficial.

In Mahabharata, there is an important dialogue between Bhishma and Yudhisthira, in which Yudhisthira desires to know about the Supreme God. Hence, Bhishma talks to him in detail about God. He describes God in 107 stanzas, which comprise around a thousand words. He explains that God is omnisciently present everywhere and is called Vishnu. Bhishma explains that the goal of all humans is dharma. He also recites the thousands of names attributed to Vishnu and states that this chanting can discard all the sins of a person. This dialogue provides numerous important details about the god. Furthermore, in 20 stanzas, Bhishma elucidates the greatness of Vishnu and his divine names. The thousand names are also known as the Vishnu Sahasranama. They are also mentioned in the Garuda Purana.

One can find countless temples in the Indian subcontinent dedicated to the different names and forms of Vishnu.

The sacred mark, called Urdhva Pundra is a tilak worn by Vishnu's devotees. Additionally, examples of icons or symbols associated with Vishnu are the gada, shankha, chakra, varamala or garland, kaustubha or the chest jewel, padma and khadga or sword.

Among the most important avatars of Vishnu is Venkateshwara. He is the principal deity of the Tirumala Venkateswara Temple in Tirupati, Andhra Pradesh. This temple is one of the most attractive cultural destinations in India. It is acknowledged as the abode of Vishnu on Earth in the Kali Yuga, as it is the place from where he supervises and guides his devotees toward moksha. In this temple, Vishnu's eyes are closed, as it is believed that the light emanating from the idol's eyes cannot be beheld by human beings.

This famous temple, dedicated to Venkateshwara, is steeped in fascinating lore and receives significant contributions from devotees. According to legend, Kubera had lent 1.4 million Ramamudra coins to Venkateshwara for his marriage to Padmavati, with the understanding that the amount would be returned within one yuga. Brahma and Shiva attested as witnesses to this event. To this date, to aid Venkateshwara in paying back his debt and to assist in the temple's management, his devotees give generous donations. It is one of India's richest temples and is known all over the world. The temple is worth more than $20 billion and receives almost $10 million annually in donations. Hence, Vishnu is considered an enabler of growth, both tangible and spiritual.

Vishnu, worshiped with numerous epithets, each representing distinct aspects of his divinity, plays a pivotal role in Hinduism. Each avatar of his is revered with distinct elements, figures and symbols, every one of them beholding unique beliefs, essence and a special relationship with Vishnu.

In the form of Padmanabha, Vishnu floats upon the limitless ocean, resting on the serpent Ananta Shesha Naga.

As Krishna, one of Vishnu's major avatars, he is known for his dark skin and playful childhood leelas,[†] embodying joy and divine love. Whereas Keshava, with his beautiful and long hair, is venerated by those seeking to avert bad luck or ill omens. As Narayana, he is the Universal Abode and the Guru of the Universe, according to the Bhagavad Gita. Madhava, the primary manifestation of Vishnu, signifies all-attractiveness and is the god of knowledge. Govinda is associated with Krishna's youthful activity as a cowherd, reflecting his role as a protector of cows. The name "Vishnu" refers to the primary preserver form, sometimes called Mahavishnu. Madhusudan, the avatar that represents Vishnu's form with a human-horse body, is hailed as "the slayer of Madhu"—he defeats the demons Madhu and Kaitabha because they had stolen the Vedas. Trivikrama, another manifestation, depicts Vishnu in his Vamana avatar, measuring the whole world in just three strides. Damodaran refers to a depiction of Krishna as a child with a rope around his belly (to keep him out of mischief), being fed by Yashoda. Purushottama, meaning the Supreme God, serves as an epithet for Krishna and, hence, Vishnu. Lastly, Hari, known as the remover of sorrow and pain, clears away darkness and illusion.

Vishnu is revered in numerous forms and names, making him the deity with the most number of temples globally. One of the most famous temples, Badrinath, the holiest shrine of Vishnu, is an integral part of the Chardham Yatra. Ranganathaswamy Temple, Srirangam, is dedicated to

---

†   A leela refers to the divine pastimes or playful activities of Krishna. These stories highlight Krishna's charming and mischievous nature during his childhood, showcasing his interactions with friends, family and the world around him.

Ranganatha, as most illustrious Vaishnava temples in south India. Other temples are the Padmanabhaswamy Temple, Tirumala Venkateswara Temple, Jagannath Puri Temple, Bhadrachalam Temple, Dwarkadhish Temple, Lakshmi Narasimhar Temple, Parashurama Temple, Laxminarayan Temple, Aswaklanta Temple, Ramanathaswamy Temple, Shrinathji Temple, Srinathji Temple, Sarangapani Temple, Vitthal Temple and Koodal Azhagar Temple.

Vishnu's most common names are Venkateshwara, Balaji, Srinivasa, Satyanarayana, Narayana, Jagannath, Padmanabha, Sridhara and the 10 avatars, which are discussed in the book's later sections.

***

Lakshmi is considered the wife of Vishnu. According to Hindu scriptures like the Vishnu Purana, the Mahabharata and the Ramayana, Lakshmi emerged during the Samudra Manthan. In this event, she chose Vishnu as her eternal consort due to his virtuous qualities and divine nature. Their union symbolizes harmony, prosperity and cosmic balance within the Hindu worldview. Lakshmi is revered as the goddess of wealth, fortune and prosperity, while Vishnu is the preserver among the Hindu Trinity. Together, they embody the ideals of marital bliss, abundance and divine grace within Hindu religious teachings and practices.

Lakshmi, whether in the form of the wife or Shakti (divine energy), is often depicted alongside Saraswati and Parvati, forming the Tridevi in Hinduism. Lakshmi is associated with good fortune in the Rigveda, while in the Atharvaveda, she is revered as the goddess of luck and prosperity. The Vishnu

Purana also teaches that Lakshmi resides where there is hard work, virtue and bravery but withdraws if these qualities fade. Lakshmi frequently accompanies Vishnu in the sojourns of all of his avatars. She appears as Sita, Rama's wife; Dharani, Parashurama's consort; and Queen Rukmini, the principal wife of Krishna, among other forms.

Out of the various mythological stories about Lakshmi, one of the most compelling ones is about the curse put on Indra by Durvasa. According to a Puranic story, Lakshmi resided in Indra's palace before he was cursed by Durvasa, a rishi who is infamous for being short-tempered. Once, the sage went to Indra's palace to give him a garland of parijata flowers. However, Indra, out of arrogance, put it around the neck of his elephant, Airavata. Durvasa was rather angered by this. He placed a curse on Indra so that he would lose his dominion over all three worlds, his wealth and riches would vanish, and even Lakshmi would abandon him. The goddess, therefore, left the realm of the gods behind and sought refuge deep inside the milky cosmic ocean. Thereafter, following many long years of the ocean getting churned by both gods and asuras who were in search of the Amrita, Lakshmi reappeared. She chose Vishnu as her eternal consort because of his noble qualities, divine attributes and his role as the preserver of the universe. Thus, Vishnu was married to Lakshmi.

In Bengali culture and other Indian folklore, Lakshmi is the daughter of Durga. She is generally portrayed with four arms, seated on a fully bloomed pinkish lotus flower. She is often depicted sitting beneath Vishnu, massaging his feet. A white owl is also shown seated close to the feet of the goddess. One of the most common names of Lakshmi is Shri. Diwali is a celebration of Lakshmi and Ganesha. Vishnu and Lakshmi are often worshiped in tandem as Lakshmi–Narayana in the temples of Vishnu.

There are many famous temples of Lakshmi like Ashtalakshmi Temple in Chennai, which is dedicated to her eight forms. They represent different aspects of prosperity and wealth. Another Ashtalakshmi Temple, also dedicated to her eight forms, is in Hyderabad and shares similar values to that of its Chennai counterpart. Mahalakshmi Temple in Mumbai, is dedicated to Mahalakshmi, also known as Amba Bai. Sripuram Golden Temple in Vellore, is famous for its golden exterior. Another famous temples is the Lakshminarayan Temple in Delhi, which is dedicated to both Lakshmi and Vishnu.

DASHAVATARA
The Incarnations of Lord Vishnu

यदा यदा हि धर्मस्य ग्लानिः भवति भारत।
अभ्युत्थानम अधर्मस्य, तदात्मानं सृजाम्यहम्।।

Yada yada hi dharmasya glanir bhavati Bharata,
Abhyutthanam adharmasya, tadatmanam srjamyaham.

Translation
Whenever evil flourishes and virtue declines,
Vishnu incarnates to save the righteous, destroy
wrong-doers and establish righteousness.
—*Bhagavad Gita, (Chapter 4, Verse 7–8)*

This shloka from the Bhagavad Gita for Vishnu states that whenever righteousness is needed, a great calamity threatens lives or evil forces threaten to rule the world, Vishnu will be reincarnated. He will establish the good, eliminate the sinister and re-establish morality. God/Vishnu will be reborn as avatars, age after age. These Vishnu avatars are mentioned in the Puranas. For example, the Bhagavata Purana lists 24 avatars. In some other Puranas like the Garuda Purana, Varaha Purana or Padma Purana, there are 10 avatars. Some Puranic narratives will simply deem a god to be an avatar, others will consider two different gods to be aspects of a single incarnation. Ten major manifestations of Vishnu are collectively known as the Dashavatar or the 10 avatars. It denotes the god's primary avatars.

Most Puranas like Agni, Varaha, Padma, Garuda, Skanda and Narada list the same avatars. Krishna and Rama are the avatars of Vishnu that are worshiped the most in present times. Out of ten, nine avatars have already covered the timespan of three yugas. One complete time cycle of Hinduism is approximately 4.32 million years. According to Hindu mythology, the last avatar, Kalki, will be born in the Kali Yuga.

Vishnu's major avatars are:

DASHAVATAR
INCARNATIONS OF LORD VISHNU

Matsya Avatar	First incarnation, in the form of a fish, to save the world	Satya Yuga
Kurma Avatar	Second incarnation, a giant tortoise, for churning the ocean	Satya Yuga
Varaha Avatar	Third incarnation, a boar, to rescue the earth from the demon Hiranyaksha	Satya Yuga
Narasimha Avatar	Fourth incarnation, a half-man, half-lion form, to protect his devotee, Prahlada	Satya Yuga
Vamana Avatar	Fifth incarnation, a dwarf Brahmin boy, to subdue the asura king Bali	Treta Yuga
Parashurama Avatar	Sixth incarnation, a Brahmin warrior who wielded an axe	Treta Yuga
Rama Chandra Avatar	Seventh incarnation, undertaken to destroy the asura king Ravana and to uphold dharma	Treta Yuga
Krishna Avatar	Eighth incarnation, manifested to restore dharma; plays a pivotal role in the Mahabharata	Dvapara Yuga
Balarama/Jagannath	A form of a wooden god along with his siblings, Balabhadra (Balarama) and Subhadra	Dvapara Yuga
Kalki Avatar	Future and the tenth incarnation, to rid the world of oppression and evil forces	Kali

Matsya Avatar or the Fish Incarnation: Matsya is depicted either as a fish or as a human-fish figure, whose torso is that of a human being. Matsya is the Sanskrit word for fish. The avatar is commonly represented with four hands: with a shankha, a chakra, one conferring a boon, and the fourth in Abhaya Mudra.

Two famous stories are associated with the Matsya avatar of Vishnu. The first involves Vishnu defeating the demons Madhu and Kaitabha to retrieve the Vedas, thereby restoring knowledge to the world. The second fascinating story narrates how Vishnu saved the Saptarishis, or the seven great sages, and all living beings from an impending flood, ensuring the continuation of life on Earth. This narrative begins with Satyavrata, also known as Vaivasvata Manu, who was a great king and devoted follower of Vishnu. One day, while Satyavrata was bathing in a pond, a small fish touched his hand and requested that he save it from getting devoured by the bigger fish. The king brought the fish to his palace in a small, oblong water pot. Once they were at his palace, he put it in a jar, but the fish grew in size. Satyavrata then put it in a bigger tank, but the fish soon outgrew that vessel as well. Looking at this, the king finally understood and asked the fish to reveal itself. Vishnu emerged and explained to Satyavrata that in the next seven days, the whole world would drown, as per the directions of Brahma. The king was therefore required to build an ark to carry herbs, varieties of seeds, the Saptarishi and their wives, along with Vasuki Naga and other animals.

Satyavrata did as instructed. As the waves swept over the land and great floods started swallowing the earth, the colossal fish, the Matsya avatar, appeared with the tremendous Vasuki Naga. The snake was used to fasten the ship to the tail of the fish. The fish swam over the floods, pulling the boat to safety, eventually reaching the top of the mighty Himalayas. Following this, the king became the first man, Manu. This was how human civilization, the one that has persisted into the present age, was reborn. This story of Vishnu, wherein he saves the earth and humans from the flood, is present in different scriptures like Brahma Purana, Bhagavata Purana, Agni Purana, Valmiki Ramayana, Aitareya Brahmana from the Rigveda, and the Mahabharata.

Kurma Avatar or the Tortoise Incarnation: Vishnu appeared in the form of a giant tortoise to churn the cosmic ocean. After a never-ending battle between devas and asuras, the former were exhausted. The asuras, on the other hand, performed austerities, received boons from Shiva and became extremely powerful. Hence, the weakened devas went to Vishnu for guidance, who explained that the only solution was to churn the cosmic ocean to obtain Amrita, the elixir of immortality. It was a formidable task. The gods could not perform it alone. Thus, they convinced the demons to assist them. But the consent of the demons was conditional, as they wanted some of the elixir too, which worried the devas as they did not want the asuras to attain immortality.

After the churning began, Vishnu transformed into a tortoise and descended to the bottom of the sea to help get the Amrita. Kurma allowed his back to serve as a pivot on which the vast mountain swung and whirled. Many objects came out because of the churning of the ocean: Shankha, a conch shell, which could ensure victory if blown during a war; Airavata, the marvelous white elephant which became Indra's vahana; Parijata, the tree that granted all wishes; Kaustubha, a jewel; Rambha, a beautiful apsara; Dhanush and other exceptional weapons; the goddess of wine, Sura, sometimes called Varuni; Lakshmi; Alakshami; Visha, the poison; and finally, Amrita, the elixir. This churning was only possible with Vishnu's help. The Kurma avatar is still worshiped in many parts of India. The Shri Kurma temple is one of the main temples where Vishnu is worshiped in the form of a tortoise.

Varaha Avatar or the Boar Incarnation: Vishnu took the appearance of a wild boar to kill the asura, Hiranyaksha, who wanted to drag Earth down to his underworld kingdom, at the bottom of the ocean. Hiranyaksha was once a gatekeeper of Vishnu's adobe, Vaikuntha. However, due to a curse, he became an asura in his subsequent life. To despoil humans and devas, Hiranyaksha grabbed Earth and immersed it in the ocean. In the story, Vishnu defeated the demon and restored Earth's position—the boar inserted his tusk into the ocean's base and lifted Earth out of the water. The Varaha avatar is portrayed as having four hands. He is half-boar, half-human and is depicted as raising Earth on his tusk.

The tale of Varaha is found in the Vedas as well. He is initially described as a form of Prajapati or Brahma, but later merged into one of the avatars of Vishnu in Puranic scriptures. The most prominent temple of Varaha is the Sri Varahaswami Temple in Tirumala, Andhra Pradesh.

Narasimha Avatar or the Lion–Man Incarnation: He is a fierce avatar of Vishnu. This half-lion and half-human was reincarnated to destroy evil, end religious persecution and calamity, and restore dharma. Narasimha is a popular deity in the Vaishnava traditions. The word Narasimha means man-lion in Sanskrit. There are references to the Narasimha avatar in different Puranas, like Bhagavata Purana, Agni Purana, Vishnu Purana, Matsya Purana, Kurma Purana and Padma Purana.

Brahma granted Hiranyakashipu, Vishnu's other sentinel turned asura, a boon, which stated that neither humans, devas nor animals would be unable to kill him. He could neither be executed by any weaponry, nor any living creature created by Brahma. Soon after receiving the new boon, he began to persecute the devotees of Vishnu. Parallelly, Hiranyakashipu had a son named Prahlada who grew up revering Narayana, a form of Vishnu. This angered Hiranyakashipu, and he tried to kill the boy. But all his attempts failed as Prahlada was guarded by Narayana.

Alternately, in the Bhagavad Gita, it is revealed that once Prahlada quarreled with Hiranyakashipu: he had declared that Vishnu was omnipresent. Hiranyakashipu retorted by asking if Vishnu was in one of the columns of the palace and struck at it hard with his hands. Instantly, Vishnu emerged in the form of Narasimha. Gripping Hiranyakashipu, the half-man, half-lion avatar sat down on the threshold to the palace, laid the king down on his thighs and with his sharp claws ripped apart the king's abdomen.

Narasimha is worshiped across India in many different ways. Some people believe him to be a calamitous form of Vishnu and, therefore, do not keep his idol at home. They maintain that he must be worshiped appropriately, as this avatar expects to be praised vigorously if one wishes to stay out of harm's way. Some of the most famous temples of Narasimha are the Shri Laxmi Narasimha Temple in Pune, Bhadrachalam Narasimha Temple in Telangana and Ahobilam Narasimha Swamy Temple in Andhra Pradesh.

Vamana Avatar or the Dwarf Incarnation: Also known as Vamanadeva, he is the dwarf reincarnation of Vishnu. Vamana means dwarf in Sanskrit. This avatar also originated in the Vedas. But it is usually associated in the Itihasas and Puranas with the legend of bringing the three worlds back together. The story goes, Bali, the king of asuras, defeated Indra in a war. Also known as Mahabali, Bali was the great-grandson of Hiranyakashipu (the one who was slain by the Narasimha avatar) and the grandson of Prahlada; he had also sired 100 heirs. Indra eventually sought aid from Vishnu, who agreed to restore him to power. To do so, Vishnu was reincarnated as Vamana, the dwarf Brahmin.

Noble-souled, Bali often offered many sacrifices, one of which was attended by Vamana. Bali felt honored by this visit and attended to the young fellow. He encouraged Vamana to ask for land, cows, precious stones, gold, anything he wished for. But Vamana said he only wanted a space of three paces that he could cover with his foot.

Shukracharya, the guru of the asuras, warned Bali about the real identity of Vamana and urged him not to go through with this gift. But Bali was ready to give away everything, as he was overwhelmed to know that Vishnu himself had come to him. As soon as he granted Vamana's request, the avatar grew in size. The dwarf became a giant. He strode over Heaven with one step, and with another, he covered Earth. For his third step, Vamana asked where he could put down his foot, and Bali offered his head. Vishnu was pleased with this, and as the Vamana avatar stepped on his head, he granted Bali moksha.

Parashurama Avatar: As Parashurama, Vishnu was also the guru of Bhishma, Dronacharya and Karna in the Mahabharata. Like the other avatars, he came to Earth when evil prevailed. This time it was because of the Kshatriyas (a Hindu caste), who with their weaponry and power had started to misuse their privilege by harming innocent people, taking their valuables by force and oppressing them. Hence, Parashurama killed the Kshatriya warriors. Despite being an avatar of Vishnu, not much is known about Parashurama.

In different texts, Parashurama is described as the fiery Brahmin who, with his axe, ended the lives of many Kshatriyas because they had abused righteous people. During the term of Parashurama, another avatar, Rama, was also incarnated. The purpose of these two avatars was different, and they each accomplished their respective goals.

Parashurama was born to the Brahmin sage Jamadagni and his Kshatriya wife, Renuka. Many legends revolve around Parashurama, and they are chiefly about his choice of weapon. Strangely enough, he even killed his mother and brothers, on the orders of his father. Parashuram was aware of his father's wrath, and he did not want to get cursed by him. He loved his mother dearly but was also a very obedient child. So, he killed his mother, and later when his father's anger had passed, he asked his father for a boon. Jamadagni was very pleased and sanctified him. Hence, his mother and brothers were brought back to life, with no memory of Parashurama having killed them. In another account, Parashurama had thrown his axe into the sea. Subsequently, the sea level started to rise. This place is presently known as the Malabar Konkan coast of Goa. A famous temple is also dedicated to Parashurama in south Goa. Parashurama Jayanti is celebrated every year on the Tritiya of the Shukla Paksha, which is the third day of the waxing moon phase in the Hindu lunar calendar. The term Shukla Paksha means bright fortnight, which is the period when the moon grows from the new moon to the full moon.

Rama Chandra Avatar: Rama Chandra was the seventh avatar of Vishnu. Like Krishna, he is one of the most popular and beloved incarnations. Krishna is embraced for his naughty capers and tender flirtations, whereas Rama is portrayed as the perfect son, brother and husband; he is the ideal king, who strictly adhered to dharma. The Rama avatar sets an example of dharmic living through his rigorous adherence to traditional roles. He was the son of Kaushalya and Dasharatha, the ruler of the kingdom of Kosala in Ayodhya. Rama was born into the Suryavansha dynasty, which later came to be known as Raghuvansha, named after King Raghu.

The main source of information about Rama comes from the famous epic Ramayana. He is the central character of the Ramayana, composed by Valmiki. The epic is made up of nearly 24,000 verses divided into 5 kandas. The story of Rama, Sita and their companions reflects on the duties, rights and social responsibilities of an individual. There are many characters in the Ramayana, but the critical ones are Dasharatha, the king of Ayodhya and Rama's father; Bharata, Lakshmana and Shatrughana, Rama's brothers; Hanuman, the devotee of Rama and a vanara from the kingdom of Kishkindha; Sugriva and Angada, allies of Rama who helped him in the war against Lanka; Ravana, the rakshasa king of Lanka; Indrajit (also known as Meghnadha), Ravana's eldest son, who defeated Rama and Lakshmana in battle twice; Kumbhakarna, Ravana's other brother, famous for his eating and sleeping habits; and Surpanakha, Ravana's rakshasi sister, who had the ability to shapeshift and the one who, infatuated with Rama, tried to seduce him.

King Dasharatha's third wife, Kaikeyi persuaded him to send Rama into exile so that her own son, Bharata, could become the king of Ayodhya. The exile lasted 14 years, during which period Ravana kidnapped Sita. Thereafter, Rama created a rescue force that included an army of vanaras and other allies.

He also built a famous bridge from the southernmost point of India's mainland to present-day Sri Lanka, which is the supposed location of Ravana's legendary kingdom. A fierce battle ensued between Rama and Ravana, where they used many deadly weapons like the Brahmastra, Gandharvastra, Chandrahasa, Varunastra, Pashupatastra and Agneyastra. Hanuman played a vital role in the Ramayana war by serving as Rama's devoted messenger and warrior. He helped rally allies, deliver important messages and fought valiantly against Ravana's forces, demonstrating immense strength and loyalty. In the end, Rama won the war and on completing his exile, he returned to Ayodhya. His return marked the celebration of Diwali, the festival of lights, a major festival for Hindus.

Most Hindus have grown up listening to the story of Rama. Additionally, Rama's life is remembered and celebrated every year with a dramatic play called Ramleela. The play follows the story of the Ramayana, along with the Ramcharitmanas narrative. Ramcharitmanas is another masterpiece, which is a part of vernacular literature, composed around the sixteenth century by the great poet Goswami Tulsidas. Consisting of seven kandas, the Awadhi poems—poems in a dialect of Hindi—in this text describe Rama's life. It is acknowledged as one of the most well-known works of Awadhi literature.

In Hindu traditions whenever a deceased person is taken to the crematorium for the last rites, a well-known chorus is recited:

राम नाम सत्य है

|| Ram Naam Satya Hai ||

The name of Ram is the truth

This phrase serves as a reminder that, while life is temporary, the divine name and truth of Ram endure forever. It reminds all those assembled that death is the only truth. It emphasizes belief in the impermanence of life and the eternal nature of truth and spirituality.

Rama was born on the ninth day of the lunar moon, Chaitra, a day which is celebrated across India as Ram Navami. Ayodhya is considered to be the birthplace of Rama; it is where the infant Rama-Lalla grew up. Based on Puranic genealogy, it is believed that Rama lived in the Treta Yuga or the second yuga, before Krishna, who was born toward the end of Dvapara Yuga.

Rama is a Vaishnav deity, who is revered at home and in temples. Some important Rama temples are the Shri Rama Janmabhoomi Temple in Ayodhya, Ramaswamy Temple in Tamil Nadu, Raghunath Temple in Jammu and Kalaram Temple in Maharashtra. The most common names of Rama are Adipurusha, Dhanurdhara and Maryada Purushottam.

Sita was the adopted daughter of King Janaka and Queen Sunayana. During her swayamvara, a grand ceremony where the woman would choose her husband, Sita selected Rama, the prince of Ayodhya. Impressed by his noble character, exceptional strength and righteousness, she was particularly drawn to his ability to string the mighty bow, a feat that showcased his extraordinary skill and made him the perfect match.

Sita had a younger sister named Urmila, and their cousins included Mandavi and Shrutakirti. Urmila found love with Lakshmana, Rama's younger brother. Mandavi married Bharata, while Shrutakirti wed Shatrughna, the youngest of Rama's brother.

Praised as the embodiment of Lakshmi, Sita exemplifies wifely devotion in the Ramayana. Interestingly, though Sita's idol is kept next to Rama's in some temples, others are exclusively dedicated to her, like Janaki Mandir in Nepal, Sita Kund in Bihar and Sita Mai Temple in Haryana.

Krishna Avatar: If protection and vengeance define the Narsimha avatar of Vishnu, and family duty and kingship are most important for Rama, then love and spirituality describe Krishna. Each avatar of his showcases different qualities, highlighting the various aspects of duty and devotion central to Hindu beliefs. One of Hinduism's favorite gods, he is popular in many regions of India and is worshiped across traditions that observe distinct perspectives. The Vaishnava groups recognize him as an avatar of Vishnu. However, according to some doctrines, Krishna is the Supreme God, Bhagavan. He is the god of empathy, love and passion. A central figure in the Mahabharata, Krishna preached the Bhagavad Gita in the epic poem, and is mentioned in various Puranas and other mythological scriptures.

One of the most famous and foremost mantra in Vaishnavism is:

ॐ नमो भगवते वासुदेवाय।
Om Namo Bhagavate Vasudevaye.

Translation
Om, I bow to Vasudev.

—Bhagavata Purana (1.5.37)

Krishna was born to Vasudeva and Devaki of the Yadava clan in Mathura. His maternal uncle, Kansa, was the king of Mathura, who was told by a fortune teller that Devaki's child would kill him. So, he tried to kill all of Devaki's children. When Krishna was born, Vasudeva secretly took the infant away, across the Yamuna River and swapped him with another child.

The legends associated to Krishna's childhood and youth describe him as a naughty cow herder who would trick his friends and family for fun. But at the same time, he charmed the people of Gokul and Vrindavan. In fact, Krishna is often represented as an enchanting, playful lover of the gopis, especially Radha. His special bond with her rendered him the name Radhakrishna. Parallelly, this butter thief was also a protector. According to a legend, Krishna lifted the Govardhana Hill to protect the inhabitants of Vrindavan from the devastating rains and floods. In another tale, a 16-year-old Krishna returned to Mathura and killed the tyrant, King Kansa. Following this, the Pandavas came into the picture. Krishna befriended Arjuna and other Pandava princes of the Kuru kingdom, and had a crucial role to play in the Kurukshetra war. One can always find a peacock feather in Krishna's hair, which represents his exuberant nature. It is a symbol of beauty and knowledge.

In the Mahabharata, Krishna agreed to become Arjuna's charioteer in the Kurukshetra war but was not allowed to use any weapons. Upon arrival at the battlefield, realizing that the enemies were his own family, Arjuna decided not to fight, and he put the Gandiva, his bow, down. Krishna then reminded him about his dharma. This conversation between Krishna and Arjuna is presented as the Bhagavad Gita in the sixth kanda of the Mahabharata. It encapsulates the essence of conscience, principles and morality.

The fateful Kurukshetra war in the Mahabharata led to the death of all 100 of Gandhari's sons. Hence, in a fit of rage and sorrow, Gandhari cursed Krishna for not preventing the war, whose impact destroyed the entire Yadava clan.

One of the most popular mantras to appease Krishna is the *Hare Krishna Maha-Mantra*:

हरे कृष्ण हरे कृष्ण, कृष्ण कृष्ण हरे हरे
हरे राम हरे राम, राम राम हरे हरे

Hare Krishna Hare Krishna, Krishna Krishna Hare Hare
Hare Rama Hare Rama, Rama Rama Hare Hare

[The Hare Krishna mantra is a chant that asks for the love and help of God, Krishna and Rama. It is used to feel closer to God and bring peace and happiness.]
—*Kali Santarana Upanishad*

One can seek the blessings of both Rama and Krishna by chanting this mantra. It gained importance during the Hare Krishna movement, brought about by the teachings of Sri Chaitanya Mahaprabhu. He is famous as the founder of the International Society for Krishna Consciousness (ISKCON).

Many forms, characters and personalities of Krishna have been presented in numerous TV shows and films over the years in India. Krishna is worshiped in multiple forms like Vasudeva, Bala Gopala, Radhakrishnan, Dwarkadheesh, Murlimanohar, Balakrishna, Keshava, Madhusudan and Muraliwale. Furthermore, there are thousands of famous temples of Krishna in India: Banke Bihari Temple in Vrindavan, Dwarkadhish Temple in Dwaraka, Krishna Balaram Mandir in Jaipur, Sri Krishna Temple in Udupi,

Nathdwara Temple in Udaipur and Venugopala Swamy Temple in Karnataka.

According to Hindu myths, Krishna's departure from Earth marked the end of the Dvapara Yuga and the beginning of the Kali Yuga. His birthday is celebrated every year as Krishna Janmashtami.

Balarama Avatar: The elder brother of Krishna is sometimes considered to be the eighth avatar of Vishnu. Narratives about Balarama are found in the Mahabharata, Bhagavata Purana, Krishna Charitmanas and a few other Puranas. Although he remained neutral in the Kurukshetra war, Balarama had taught the skills of warfare to both Duryodhana and Bhima. He ensured that none broke the laws of war. He is also known as Baladeva, Haladhara, Balabhadra and Halayudha. Additionally, Balarama is a significant god in the Jagannath tradition.

People often wonder why the Jagannath tradition is so famous and unique compared to other sects of worship for the incarnations of Vishnu. This is so because Jagannath is only his abstract representation. The figure of Jagannath is a wooden piece with an asymmetrical face and huge circular eyes. This icon, sometimes, does not even have hands or legs. He is considered a manifestation of Vishnu but not an avatar like Rama or Krishna.

The Sanskrit word Jagannath means "lord of the world." In fact, the English word "juggernaut," which means unstoppable, originated from this deity's name. Furthermore, Jagannath is a significant god in regional Indian states like Odisha, Chhattisgarh, West Bengal, Jharkhand, Bihar, Gujarat, Assam, Manipur and Tripura. Shri Jagannath Puri in Odisha is a great shrine and one of the most sacred places for worshiping him. The triad of deities worshiped in this temple includes Jagannath, his brother Balabhadra and sister Subhadra.

Interestingly, in his temples, it is believed that the idols of Jagannath are partially incomplete. There is a popular legend behind the unfinished idol. In the Satya Yuga, a king named Indradyumna was born. He was an exceptional devotee of Vishnu and wanted to build a temple for the god. On one occasion, Vishnu appeared in his dreams and advised him to go to Banki Muhana (a temple near the river) and find a big log of wood from a neem tree, growing along the bank of the river. He told Indradyumna to use that trunk to create the idol. The king decoded the meaning of his dream and found the log of wood. Soon, he invited all the craftsmen in his kingdom to make the statue. Many tried, but it was all in vain. Finally, Vishwakarma appeared as a craftsman and proposed making the idol on one condition: he stated that no one should interrupt him until the carving was complete. The king agreed and Vishwakarma chose to work behind the closed doors of the temple. But months passed and he did not open the door. King Indradyumna grew restless. Finally, unable to quash the feelings of apprehension, he decided to check on the progress of the idol's creation. When he opened the doors, he found three incomplete statues, and no Vishwakarma in sight. This lore serves as the basis for unfinished statues of Vishnu being worshiped, along with those of his brother and sister.

Additionally, in the Banki Muhana temple, the idol is worshiped inside and taken out only once a year for nine days. Every year, a chariot festival, commonly known as Jagannath Ratha Yatra, is held in Puri, Odisha. In this festival, millions of devotees come together to celebrate and get a glimpse of the god. For this occasion, three enormous chariots for Jagannath,

Balabhadra and Subhadra are constructed every year using the logs of a specific and unique neem tree. They are decorated beautifully. The chariots' construction commences on Akshaya Tritiya, the third day of the bright fortnight of Vaisakha, with an agni yagna ritual. Following this, the three gods are carried out of the temple. The gods visit another temple and stay there for nine days. The three chariots have been decorated in the same fashion for thousands of years now. Some other major festivals celebrated by the devotees are Snana Yatra, Dola Yatra, Chandana Yatra and Hari Sayan.

Kalki Avatar: Kalki is the proposed tenth avatar of Vishnu. His birth is foretold to be at the end of the Kali Yuga, the final yuga, which would supposedly bring an end to the endless cycle of life and death. It is believed that Kalki will bring an end to the darkest era—Kali Yuga. The name Kalki is derived from the word "Kaal," which means time. There are no details of the Kalki avatar in Vedic literature. In fact, the description and details about the avatar vary across the Puranas. This avatar is also mentioned in the Mahabharata, and in the Mahapuranas, such as Vishnu Purana, Matsya Purana and Bhagavata Purana. These sources state that there will be several ways to identify the Kalki avatar: he will be a warrior who will have the power to mold the direction of time and restore the divine path; he will have several extraordinary weapons, like the Ratnamaru, which he will be awarded by Shiva himself. According to the mythic lores, Kalki will have the power to change the wheel of dharma. This warrior will fight many wars, and the battles will be inevitable.

LORD SHIVA AND GODDESS PARVATI

Shiva, the third principal deity of the Hindu trinity, is known as the destroyer. Three eyes, a blue neck, a crescent moon adorning his hair and a garland of skulls or serpents around his neck: these are some of his distinctive features. His body is adorned with pale ash from cremation grounds. Nandi, the bull, serves as Shiva's vahana, and its idol is also commonly found in the deity's temples.

The name Shiva is not mentioned in any of the Vedas. Instead it is Rudra, a common name of his, that first appeared in the Rigveda. In the text, Rudra is used with reference to Agni and is sometimes also known as the god of yagnas. He is an important god for diseases, remedies, sins and healing. Many hymns attributed to Rudra are used to promote the recovery of men and women, as well as animals such as horses and cows. He is also the god of nourishment. The Brahmanas narrate a tale about Rudra: Once, when he was an infant, he was weeping. When his father, Prajapati, enquired about the reason, Rudra said he was crying because he had no name. So his father gave him the title "Rud," which means "to weep" in Sanskrit. In the Yajurveda, Satarugriya, a long hymn, appeals to Rudra using multiple epithets. He is described in this hymn as someone with red skin, a blue neck and 1,000 eyes. Rudra, from the Vedas, transformed for eons into the great and powerful, Shiva. Shaivism is a significant Hindu religious sect that regards Shiva as the ultimate and supreme deity to be worshiped. He represents time—endless and inexorable.

Shiva is often portrayed as an ascetic yogi, abstaining from all worldly pleasures, but he is also depicted as tied within the bonds of marriage. Therefore, he is shown meditating and residing on Mount Kailash and, at times, also represented as a passive god with his consort Uma (also known as Uma-Maheshwari) and son Skanda (sometimes known as Somaskanda). At times, Shiva is the divine dancer Natesa/Nataraja. On other occasions, he embodies a half-male and half-female form as Ardhanarishvara. Another form arises as a result of Vishnu and Shiva coming together as Harihara. Shiva is the god of cattle in the form of Pashupatinath. He is the chief of the gods as Mahadev, the slaughterer of beasts as Samharamurtis and a yoga teacher as Yoga Dakshinamurti. As Bhutesvara, Shiva becomes the god of ghosts, dwarfs and goblins—in this form, he lives in cemeteries or similar places, wearing a necklace made of skulls. Another representation of his is the lingam, also known as shivalinga. The lingam is a short cylindrical pillar-like symbol, made of stone, metal, gemstone, clay or other material. The lingam represents one of the oldest forms of worshiping Shiva. In fact, some of the oldest lingams are dated earlier than 2300 BCE.

Shiva is the most extraordinary yogi. He is wild and fierce. He is the god of destruction. But concurrently, he is soft, lovable and charming. With his multitudinous yet fluid forms and manifestations, he can be distinguished from the other Hindu gods.

Every form of Shiva is worshiped because each of them represents a specific aspect of his divine attributes and cosmic responsibilities. All these forms have particular symbolisms attached to them and are revered according to local customs and beliefs. Moreover, devotees often develop a personal affinity toward a particular form of his, based on their spiritual journey, experiences or specific needs for guidance and support. Out of this deity's numerous forms, some unique manifestations are mentioned below:

Bhikshatana: This manifestation is portrayed as the divine beggar. In this form, Shiva is depicted as a nude, four-armed god with ornaments, with a cobra coiled around his neck, a bowl in one of his hands, a drum in another and a dog by his side. As Bhikshatana, Shiva atones for his sins. The great ascetic compensates for cutting off the fifth head of Brahma or for killing Vishnu's sentinels. This form is popular in south India but is lesser known in the northern states. The manifestation is narrated in many south Indian texts like Skanda Purana. All in all, though, Shiva is rarely worshiped in this form.

Mukhalinga: The lingam is abstract and aniconic. This is the oldest iconographic form of worship, and is mentioned in the Upanishads, Puranas, the Ramayana and the Mahabharata. This short cylindrical form is how Shiva is mostly worshiped in the modern day. The lingam found in the ancient period sometimes have the face of Shiva carved on it, and are called Mukhalinga, which can be made of stone or metal. It is placed on top of the shivalinga. It can have one, four, five or even a thousand faces. The one-faced Mukhalinga is called the Eka-mukhalinga, the five-faced variant is called Pancha-mukhalinga and the thousand-faced one is called Sahasra-linga.

Vinadhara: This form of Shiva represents the god of music. Vinadhara is depicted as listening to himself play the lute or veena. Additionally, this manifestation is often shown in a yoga posture, holding a veena and sometimes even the Trishul. Vinadhara Shiva is soft, endearing and charming. When in this form, he is portrayed as sitting under a banyan tree, facing south—this is called the Dakshinamurthy aspect of Shiva.

Gangadhara: Shiva's epithet Gangadhara signifies his role as the bearer of the Ganga River. When Ganga descended to Earth, he received her in the coils of his matted hair, which slowed her downward stream and allowed her to flow gently on the mortal realm. This act not only saved Earth from the impact of Ganga's force but also purified the river, making it sacred. Hence, Shiva became known as Gangadhara, which means "one who holds or supports the Ganga."

Gajasurasamhara: This is a fierce aspect of Shiva, who is the destroyer of the elephant demon, Gajasura. Gajasura was an asura who did strict penance and gained strength and a boon from Brahma. Soon after gaining the blessing, he committed atrocities because of which Shiva had to intercede and kill him. Hence, Shiva is also portrayed as Gajasurasamhara. The icon of this form was famous in medieval India, where he is shown with 8–16 arms, holding a trident, a sword, an elephant's tusk, a shield, a bell and elephant skin. On his side, Parvati stands, along with Kartikeya, the god of war, and Ganesha. The goddess is, in fact, fearful of this aspect of Shiva.

In addition to the forms mentioned above, Shiva embodies various other, equally significant forms with unique names and distinct representations. The Shiva

Sahasranama lists over a thousand names ascribed to him, many of which describe his attributes, such as Nilakantha or the blue-throated one, and Trilocana or the three-eyed one. Additional well-known forms include Nataraja, Ardhanarishvara, Kalabhairava and Chandrashekhara. Furthermore, commonly used names for Shiva include Shambhu, Shankara, Mahesha and Mahadeva. These forms and names highlight different aspects of his divine nature and cosmic responsibilities within the religion.

Shiva is undoubtedly one of the most distinct Hindu deities, who possesses unique attributes that distinguish him from other Hindu gods. But what is it that sets him apart from other deities?

Some of the fascinating characteristics that make him truly one of a kind are:

The Third Eye: Symbolizes insight, wisdom and the ability to see beyond the physical realm. It represents the destruction of ignorance and illusion, and the illumination of the truth. When activated, it unleashes immense energy and power, often associated with the transformation and destruction of evil.

Crescent Moon: Shiva bears on his head the crescent moon. Due to this feature, the epithet "Chandrashekhar," is attributed to him, which points to having the moon as his crest.

Ashes: The iconography for Shiva shows his body coated with ashes called vibhuti. Three lines of white ash are drawn horizontally across his forehead.

Blue Throat: Shiva drank the poison churned up by the Samudra Manthan, to eliminate the destructive capacity of the ocean and stored it in his neck. This earned him the name Nilakantha.

Tiger Skin: Shiva is often shown seated on a tiger skin because it symbolizes his mastery over the forces of nature and his ability to transcend them. The tiger skin also represents his role as a renunciant and ascetic, as well as his connection with the wilderness and primal energy.

Serpent Necklace: Shiva is often garlanded with a serpent. Some legends state that the serpent symbolizes his powers of destruction and recreation. Wearing the serpent also suggests his transcendence beyond mortality.

Drum: A small, hourglass-shaped drum with two heads, called the damaru, is also part of his ensemble. The damaru is believed to represent the primordial sound from which creation emerged. Shiva's drumbeats symbolize the rhythmic creation and dissolution of the universe.

Shiva is worshiped not only by humans but also by demons, ghosts and hobgoblins. If we try to estimate the sum of him and his family's devotees, they would turn out to be the most worshiped gods in Hinduism. In fact, the shivlinga is also worshiped along with the other members of his family—one can always witness Ganesha, Kartikeya, Parvati, Nandi and other idols of the Shiva family placed near the shivlinga in the temple. Most of Shiva's legends center around his consort, as well as his and Parvati's sons and daughters.

People worship Shiva because he destroys ignorance and negativity. Worshiping him is about finding spiritual wisdom, inner calm and freedom from worldly desires. Shiva, known for meditation and self-discipline, encourages his followers to reflect upon themselves and seek inner truth. He is also seen as the guardian who gives blessings, removes obstacles and grants wishes. Worshiping him is a way to grow spiritually, find harmony between creation and change, and seek divine blessings and good fortune.

***

Parvati is the consort of Shiva, and the mother of Ganesha and Kartikeya. She is also known as Gauri or Uma. According to the Puranas, she is the sister of the river goddess Ganga, and that of the preserver, Vishnu. She is named after her father, King Himavan, also called King Parvat; "Parvata" is the Sanskrit word for mountain. He is considered the god of mountains and personifies the Himalayas. The name Parvati is mentioned in Puranic scriptures but not in the Vedic ones. However, the Ramayana and the Mahabharata present Parvati as Shiva's wife. She was a princess, and her wedding to Shiva, the Adiyogi, was a grand affair.

Like Shiva, Parvati embodies both gentle and fierce aspects. She represents the divine feminine and is often depicted as a beautiful and benevolent woman. Parvati's power reflects the unity of male and female energies. When presented alongside Shiva, she is depicted with two arms but can have four when shown alone. A yoni and linga together often symbolize Parvati and Shiva. Yoni means "womb or the place of gestation," and the yoni–linga union symbolizes the origin, source or regenerative power.

In the Puranas, it is stated that after their marriage, Parvati moved to Mount Kailash, the abode of Shiva. In Hindu legends, she is the ideal wife, mother and homemaker. Though Parvati is often worshiped as an individual deity, temples dedicated solely to the goddess are rare. So, most of her images come from temples devoted to her husband. We'll explore more about Parvati in the upcoming section on the goddesses of Hinduism.

THE CHILDREN OF LORD SHIVA

It is believed that Shiva had two sons. However, according to several Puranic scriptures, he had five sons and three daughters. Ganesha and Kartikeya are the most prominent and frequently worshiped among the five sons.

Ganesha, also known as Vinayaka, is one of the most renowned deities in the present Hindu pantheon. In the Vedas, he emerged as a deity around first century CE. "Gana" means "people" and "Isha" means "lord" in Sanskrit. Hence, Ganesha means "lord of the ganas" or "lord of people." The name Ganesha is primarily used in north India, while in south India, he is known as Ganapati. Although the name Ganapati appears in the Rigveda, it refers to Brihaspati, the lord of speech and wisdom. In later texts, however, Ganapati becomes associated with Ganesha, highlighting his connections to knowledge and learning.

As Ganesha embodies prosperity, he is one of the most revered gods. He is renowned outside India too, in countries like Nepal, Sri Lanka, Bali, Thailand, Fiji and Mauritius, but with different names. His distinct appearance makes him easy to recognize because he is the god with an elephant head, a potbelly and big ears. His large ears make sure that he hears everyone's distress. He holds a modak (a sweet dumpling), an axe or a noose, a lotus and a goad in his four hands. The axe /noose symbolizes the annihilation of obstacles. The lotus represents refined knowledge, which symbolizes detachment from the material world. The goad is the instrument via which Ganesha propels humankind to achieve their goals, and the modak is a symbol of happiness and cheerfulness. His vahana is a rat, and there is a lot of food at his feet, which signifies wealth and power. The most common food offered to Ganesha includes modak and shrikhand—a sweet dish made of yogurt and motichoor laddoo, a popular Indian sweet made from tiny fried balls of gram flour soaked in sugar syrup.

Puranic tales present different versions of Ganesha. The Shiva Purana narrates a story about the origin of Ganesha. Once, Parvati ordered Nandi, the chief guard at Shiva's abode, to prevent anyone from entering her palace, as she was bathing. When Shiva reached the palace's entrance, Nandi did not stop him. Consequently, Parvati was not amused. So, she created a boy's idol from mud, gave him life and empowered him with the essential powers to challenge anybody. After some time, Shiva returned home. The boy followed Parvati's instructions and forbade him to enter the premises. Shiva tried to convince the boy, but it was in vain. Irritated, he beheaded the boy. When Parvati came back from her bath, she was furious. She asked the god to resurrect the boy. Shiva ordered Shiva-Ganas, his attendants who lived on Mount Kailash, to find someone sleeping with their head facing the north, as a head was required to restore the boy's life. The Shiva-Ganas came across an elephant. Hence, Shiva affixed the elephant's head to the boy's body and he came to be known as Ganesha.

Furthermore, one peculiarity about the elephant head is that it has only one tusk intact, while the other one is broken. Ganesha holds the broken tusk in his hand, and many idols depict this detail. The broken tusk holds another tale. On one occasion, when Parashurama, an avatar of Vishnu, had gone to visit Shiva, Ganesha blocked his entrance as his father was asleep. A fight erupted, and when Ganesha and Parashurama were engaged in a battle, the rishi threw his axe at Ganesha. He identified it as his father's weapon, which Shiva had given to the rishi. Hence, he received it with reverence upon one of his tusks, which was then chopped off. Hence, he is also known as Ekdant, which means "with one tusk." Thus, the elephant head is an emblem of wisdom, coupled by the fact that Ganesha's vahana, the rat, symbolizes perseverance. Hence, the god has become the embodiment of success.

According to a famous story, Veda Vyasa, a revered rishi, asked Ganesha to write the epic Mahabharata, and the wise elephant-headed god agreed, but only after putting forth a unique condition. Ganesha vowed to write the epic, but only if the sage could recite it without pause. Veda Vyasa accepted the challenge, but demanded, in turn, that Ganesha must understand each verse before writing it down. Thus, as the sage recited the verses, Ganesha absorbed their meaning and quickly wrote them down. This is how the great Indian epic, Mahabharata, came into being. Therefore, even today, Ganesha is revered by scholars, financiers, writers and businesspeople alike, for his wisdom and intellect.

In Hinduism, no auspicious occasion can start without seeking Ganesha's blessings. Sagacious and prudent, he is the god of good opportunities and auspicious beginnings. In almost every house, shop, hospital and office in India, one can find his idol. One of the most chanted mantras of Ganesha is:

॥ वक्रतुण्ड महाकाय सूर्यकोटि समप्रभ ।
निर्विघ्नं कुरु मे देव सर्वकार्येषु सर्वदा ॥

Vakratunda Mahakaya, Surya Koti Samaprabaha,
Nirvighnam Kurumedeva, Sarva Karyeshu Sarvada.

Translation

O Ganesha, with a large body and a curved
trunk, radiant like a million suns, please remove
all obstacles from all my endeavors, always.

—*Ganesha Stotras*

The primary texts about Ganesha are the Ganesha Purana, the Mudgala Purana and the Ganapati Atharvashirsa. This deva of intellect and wisdom is admired as the remover of hindrances. In the Ganapatya tradition, a specific sect of Hinduism, Ganesha is the supreme deity. The Hindu title of respect, 'Shri,' is often added before his name. This salutation to Ganesha is found at the beginning of every sacred book, literature and wedding invitation card: *Shri Ganeshay Namah.*

Large and striking idols of the god can be seen in many temples across India. Some of the most popular and well-known temples of Ganesha that attract pilgrims from all over India are Siddhivinayak Temple in Mumbai and Shri Ganpatipule Temple in Ratnagiri. In fact, the oldest temple dedicated to him is in Ranthambore's 700-year-old fort.[16]

Ganesh Chaturthi, the most important festival dedicated to the deity, is celebrated across India.

***

On a parallel note, Kartikeya or Murugan is the eldest son of Shiva and Parvati. Kartikeya is the god of war and is also recognized as Skanda and Subrahmanya. He is an ancient god, whose origins can be traced back to the Vedic era. His likeness is found in many medieval temples all over India, such as the one in the Ellora and the Elephanta caves. Murugan is one of the primary deities in the temples of Tamil Nadu, India and Sri Lanka. He is recognized as the god of the Tamil language and is mentioned in several texts in the Sangam literature of south India. Some of the busiest temples of south India are dedicated to him. All the six abodes of Murugan are in Tamil Nadu, and each of these temples relay a different tale.

Kartikeya is also glorified as Subrahmanya, which means "devotional or favorable to Brahmins." Kartikeya is mentioned in the Shiv Purana. His iconography varies significantly and sometimes he is typically represented as an ever-youthful man, riding or standing near a peacock. He is portrayed with a varying number of heads, ranging from one to six. He is famous for winning the war against the asura Taraka. Other names of Kartikeya include: Aaiyyan, Cheyyon, Senthil, Swaminatha, Arumugam, Sanmukh, Dandapani, Kadhirvelan, Kandhan, Vishakha and Mahasena.

Apart from Ganesha and Kartikeya, Shiva has three other sons: Ayyappa, Andhaka and Bhauma, who are lesser-known but equally fascinating figures in the pantheon. Ayyappa, who was born when Shiva married Mohini, is highly revered in

Kerala and other parts of south India. Andhaka, the second son of Shiva, was raised by an asura named Hiranyaksha and was born blind. In some folklore, Shiva killed Andhaka, as he posed to be his father's biggest opponent. Bhauma, the third son of Shiva, was raised by Bhumi. Named after his mother, he remains largely forgotten. Additionally, Shiva and Parvati had three daughters—Ashok Sundari, Jyoti and Manasa. Ashok Sundari is associated with the removal of sorrows, Jyoti symbolizes light and brilliance, and Manasa is often regarded as the goddess of the mind and emotions. Each daughter represents different aspects of life and spirituality. These lesser-known children of Shiva add to the richness and complexity of Hinduism, and their stories can be fascinating to explore.

DEVIS

The Goddesses of Hinduism

"Devi" in Sanskrit means goddess. It is similar to the male form "deva," which means god. The female energy, the Eternal Goddess or doctrine of power, has always been God's counterpart in Hinduism. The Goddess has a distinct type of worship ascribed to her. She has a specific set of devotees. In a major sect of Hinduism, called Shaktism, the metaphysical reality is considered Shakti or a woman. She is regarded as the Supreme Being. The most familiar forms of Devi found in Shaktism are Durga, Kali, Saraswati, Lakshmi, Parvati and Tripurasundari.

However, the Vedas include numerous Goddesses, such as Parvati, Prithvi, Aditi, Nirrti, Ratri, Aranyani, Raka, Puramdhi, Bharati and Mahi. In the Vedas, Devi is mentioned in the Devi Upanishad as Brahman, in which she is the chief deity. All prayers are offered to her. Even Mother Earth is called Bhumi Maa. Goddesses such as Shakti, Lakshmi, Parvati, Saraswati, Sita, Radha, Durga, Kali and Sati have been revered since the Puranic period. The seventh book of the Devi Bhagavata Purana details the theology of Shaktism. Inspired by the Bhagavad Gita, this book is called the Devi Gita.

Shakti, the goddess of power, energy and strength, is primarily identified as Parvati, the wife and consort of Shiva. Her other forms are Durga and Kali. Vedic literature does not have any specific goddess who matches the conceptualization of Durga. The legends of the angry and ferocious form of Parvati formulate the Durga and Kali avatars. Parvati is a gentle, faithful and traditional woman, but she exhibits a contrasting form when she appears as Durga or Kali.

We have seen that the goddesses from the Puranic period are usually worshiped alongside their male counterparts, like Brahma, Vishnu or Shiva. However, the goddesses have a substantial following of their own, too. There are many temples dedicated to the different forms of Devi and the ancient texts recount several tales about them. Many Hindu scriptures mention that cycles of creation and destruction of the world have happened multiple times in the past. Once, after such a period of destruction, Vishnu performed great austerities to appease Sati, for only she was capable of re-creating the world. To help Vishnu, she incarnated in different avatars and re-created Earth. Sati, or Kushmanda as she was called in this form, gave birth to the universe in the form of a cosmic egg.

Durga is the chief—and a very popular—avatar of Parvati. A pure form of Shakti, she manifests as the protector of the universe. She is depicted as sitting on a lion. Various portrayals of the goddess show arms that range anywhere between 8–18 in number, carrying weapons like bow and arrows, a thunderbolt, a sword and a beautiful discus. Like Shiva, Durga has also been called Triyambake, meaning "the three-eyed goddess." She is also the goddess of battle, the warrior form of Parvati. There is an interesting tale of a fierce battle between Durga with Mahishasura, an asura who earned the favor of Shiva after a long and hard penance. Durga was created by Brahma, Vishnu and Shiva, who were not strong enough to defeat the demon. To slaughter Mahishasura, the triad combined their energy and created Durga. Her essence is borrowed from the male divinities as she is the true source of their inner energy. Durga fought with Mahishasura for over 15 days. The demon kept changing his physical appearance during the battle to an animal, human and even a bird, and tried to mislead her. Eventually, when he transformed into a buffalo, Durga pierced him with her trident. Durga's triumph over Mahishasura represents the victory of good over evil, highlighting her strength and protective qualities. As a goddess, she is also worshiped as the Supreme Being and the creator of the universe. The legends of Durga appear in the Mahabharata, the Ramayana and the Puranas.

Furthermore, there are many epithets for Durga in Shaktism. She is revered for nine other manifestations called

Navadurga, which include: Shailaputri, Brahmacharini, Chandraghanta, Kushmanda, Skandamata, Katyayini, Kaalratri, Mahagauri and Siddhidatri. She is worshiped for nine consecutive days during Navaratri. Her temples are especially prevalent in the eastern and northeastern parts of the Indian subcontinent. It is said that one of the best ways to appease Durga is by chanting her mantras. The most common of those mantras is:

सर्व मंगला मांगल्ये शिवे सर्वार्थ साधिके।
सरण्ये त्र्यम्बके गौरि नारायणि नमोऽस्तु ते॥

Sarva Mangala Mangalye Shive Sarvartha Sadhike,
Saranye Trayambike Gauri Narayani Namostute.

Translation

You are the most auspicious of all the devis. You are pure and holy, and protect those who surrender to you. You are also known as the mother of the three worlds and are Gauri, daughter of the mountain king. We repeatedly bow down to the mother and offer our devotion.

—*Durga Suktam*

The notable festivals that honor her are Durga Puja, Dashain and Navaratri. One of the most important festivals of eastern India, especially West Bengal, Durga Puja is celebrated by venerating attractive and colorful clay idols of the goddess (that are generally placed in massive pandals for the public to behold). These idols are worshiped for nine days, after which they are carried out on the streets, accompanied by singing and dancing, for their immersion in a body of water. The day of Durga's triumph is lauded as Vijayadashami, Dashain or Dussehra, another major festival in India.

Across the country, out of the several temples dedicated to the goddess, some are more important than others. These include Vaishno Devi Temple in Jammu and Kashmir, Mansa Devi Temple in Uttarakhand, Chamunda Devi Temple in Himachal Pradesh, Kamakhya Temple in Assam, Maa Jwalamukhi Temple in Himachal Pradesh, Karni Mata Temple in Rajasthan, Chamundeshwari Temple in Karnataka and Naina Devi Temple in Uttarakhand.

Kali or Mahakali is another one of the most dominant forms of Shakti. She is depicted as a ruthless and fearless goddess, mostly in two forms: Kali with four arms, or as Mahakali with 10 arms. She is portrayed with blue or black skin. In the Mahakali form, she holds a sword in one of her 10 hands and the chopped head of the asura, Raktbija, in another; she adorns a garland made of 52 skulls and wears a skirt made of the dismembered arms of demons. Raktabija had been granted a boon—should even a single drop of his blood fall to the ground, it would give rise to a new demon of his exact kind. To prevent this catastrophe from happening, Kali sucked all the blood from the demon until he was lifeless.

Kali is also the chief of the Mahavidyas, a group of 10 Tantric goddesses. The Mahavidyas emerged in the post-Puranic period, around sixth century ce. Mahavidyas, meaning "the great pearls of wisdom," include the goddess's 10 forms: Kali, Tara, Tripura Sundari, Bhuvaneshvari, Bhairavi, Chhinnamasta, Dhumavati, Bagalamukhi, Matangi and

Kamala. In fact, Kali is said to have 12, and sometimes more than 20, different embodiments.

In some depictions, Kali stepping out with her left foot represents breaking free from traditional rules and societal limits. Additionally, the Samhara manifestation of Kali is her most dangerous and powerful form. She is the chief goddess as per the Tantric texts. She represents the death and destruction aspect of Kali and is majorly worshiped by the tantric tradition of Hinduism.

The figure of Kali is perceived as that of a destroyer of sinners and demons. According to a famous anecdote, after defeating the asura, she began to dance, and the earth started shaking and crumbling. Shiva requested Kali to stop, but in her excitement, she paid him no heed. As a last resort, Shiva lay down on the ground, and as she danced, Kali inadvertently stepped on his chest. Realizing the gravity of the situation, she stuck out her tongue in surprise. This gesture is often interpreted as a symbol of her fierce nature rather than restraint. Most renditions of the story highlight this moment, emphasizing her realization and untamed spirit.

Moreover, Kali represents female empowerment and liberation. Her actions signify the strength of feminine energy, the breaking of societal norms and the assertion of autonomy. It's also essential to recognize how Kali embodies the power to challenge conventions and reclaim one's identity.

In the late medieval period, Kali was also associated with animal sacrifice. It is believed that even today, in certain remote villages, especially in Nepal, sacrifices are performed secretly at the shrines of Kali or Durga.

These are just a few examples, as Hinduism venerates multiple goddesses, each embodying different aspects and powers. They play integral roles in spiritual and cultural life, representing the various facets of existence and divine energies of this religion.

LORD HANUMAN
The Valiant and Gigantic God of Monkeys

Hanuman is another famous god from the epic Ramayana. He is not just the companion but the greatest devotee of Rama. Hanuman is also mentioned in the Mahabharata and other Puranas, which were written after the Ramayana. He is the son of Vayu. According to Hindu legends, Hanuman was born to Anjana and Kesari. Anjana, a beautiful apsara from the celestial court of Brahma, was cursed by a sage to turn into a monkey. Brahma could not remove the curse, but he helped Anjana by promising her that she would be reborn on Earth, where she would get married to the Monkey King. Thereafter, being an ardent devotee of Shiva, she performed a strict penance to please him. Shiva was impressed and granted her a boon—he prophesied that her son, the great Hanuman, Pawan Putra or the son of Vayu, would free her from the curse.

Hanuman is one of Hinduism's unusual gods, worshiped by almost all the sects like Vaishnavism, Shaivism and Shaktism. Hanuman is likewise considered an incarnation of Shiva, as he exemplifies great strength, devotion and perseverance.

During the medieval period in India, the worship of Hanuman was quite prevalent. It is said that Hanuman can deliver anything to anyone, if he is approached with generosity. This belief is reflected in the renowned *Hanuman Chalisa*, composed of 40 verses dedicated to him. The hymn was written by the exceptional Vaishnava poet and devotee of Rama, Goswami Tulsidas, who would frequently call out to Hanuman or think of him whenever he faced any distress or pain. And Hanuman always seemed to help him.

The Hanuman Chalisa is composed in the Awadhi language and is one of the most interesting devotional hymns recited by millions of Hindus every day. This hymn is a testament to the faith and devotion of countless individuals, who have found solace and comfort in his unwavering assistance.

There are numerous motivating narratives associated with Hanuman, which are incredibly, and particularly, famous among children. One such story is of Hanuman's childhood. As a child, he grew more powerful than any other child of his age. His appetite grew at a similar pace, and his mother had difficulty finding enough food to feed him. One day, when Hanuman asked his mother for food, she told him that he could eat the fruits from the trees in the forest. After devouring all the fruits, the child got confused by the yellowish-red sun. His young mind thought it was a big fruit that could surely satisfy his hunger. Aided by his formidable powers, he jumped high into the sky, grew to a gigantic size and attempted to swallow the sun. This caused sudden darkness to fall all around, making all the gods fearful of the child. Later, after they pleaded to Hanuman, he released the sun back into the sky. Brihaspati, the wise priest of the gods, explained to Hanuman's mother that for the time being her son would forget his powers because the gods and the sages willed it so. But in the future, at exactly the right moment and only when someone reminded him of his divine abilities, he'll regain his memories of his powers and be able to use them again.

Sundar Kanda is the fifth volume in the Ramayana, which concentrates on Hanuman. His story coincides with Rama's in the latter's last year of the 14-year exile. Hanuman helped Rama rescue Sita. Whenever the Ramayana is staged as a play, after Rama, it is the role of Hanuman that is considered to be one of the most important parts.

Hanuman mostly appears as a monkey figure with a red face, standing erect like a human. He is sometimes depicted mid-air, flying while holding a massive mountain in his hand. He is mainly worshiped alongside Rama and one can always find an idol of Hanuman in a temple dedicated to Rama. Still, there are shrines dedicated exclusively to Hanuman that are famous and are visited by thousands of pilgrims every year, throughout India.

One of the stories about Hanuman goes like this: One time, Hanuman saw Sita putting sindoor (vermilion) on her forehead. A confused Hanuman asked what she was doing. Sita explained that the sindoor was a sign of her love and respect for Rama. Hearing this, Hanuman applied the red vermilion all over his body to impress Rama. This is the reason why the idols of Hanuman are painted with sindoor.

Hanuman is among the most revered gods in Hinduism, symbolizing strength, courage and devotion. He is worshiped under various names such as Sankat Mochan, meaning "the one who removes all troubles," Bajrang Bali, Mahavir, Mahabir and many more.

Furthermore, Tuesday is the day of the week dedicated to his worship—it is a popular custom among his devotees to pray to him on this day in order to seek his blessings. They believe that worshiping Hanuman on Tuesdays can help them overcome all obstacles and difficulties in life. Devotees also believe that reciting the Hanuman Chalisa brings good luck and prosperity. Many people keep a picture or a statue of Hanuman in their homes or offices as a symbol of strength and protection. The Sankat Mochan Hanuman Temple in Varanasi is the most famous temple dedicated to him and is believed to have been built at the spot where Hanuman appeared to Tulsidas, who later went on to compose the Hanuman Chalisa.

ANCESTORS, SPIRITS AND THE WORSHIPING OF ASURAS

A puzzling question often arises in discussions regarding Hinduism: why are demons or asuras worshiped in this religion?

For instance, both the gentle Parvati and her fierce form, Kali, are equally revered. Kali, often seen as the goddess of war and death, represents violence and power. She is depicted with dark blue or black skin and sunken eyes; she dons a tiger skin and a garland of human heads, and in one of her hands she holds a demon's blood-dripping head. Kali symbolizes the wild and untamed aspects of the divine. Similarly, shadow planets like Rahu and Ketu‡ are also objects of worship. While Surya and Chandra receive offerings, planets like Rahu, Ketu and Shani, known

---

‡　Two of the Navagraha or nine major celestial bodies, are considered shadow planets.

for bringing bad luck, are appeased with yagnas. Ancient texts illustrate how these evil forces can bring about hardships, such as health issues, diseases and even death.

The worship of asuras in Hinduism is a complex practice, encompassing fear, respect and an understanding of the universe's need for balance. This tradition reflects the diverse beliefs within Hinduism, where both good and evil are integral to the spiritual journey of an individual and the cosmos. The primary motivation for this kind of worship is based on fear and acknowledging the influence these entities possess. Even the great gods of Hinduism encounter malign spirits in numerous tales. This amalgamation of divine and demonic forces demonstrates a profound comprehension of the universe's equilibrium, where light and darkness, good and evil, are all fundamental aspects of existence. Through these narratives and traditions, Hinduism imparts the idea that managing these forces is an essential aspect of the spiritual journey, steering believers toward a harmonious life.

Demonic forces, such as asuras and other evil entities, have existed in Hindu lore since the early days of the religion. Notable examples include Vritra, the serpent-like asura, and Namuchi, the powerful rakshasa, both mentioned in the Rigveda. Several hymns within the Rigveda are dedicated to Indra's victory over Vritra, illustrating his power and courage. Powerful asura king Ravana, renowned for his wisdom, wealth and strength, is portrayed as a villain in the Ramayana. Hiranyakashipu, a powerful demon defeated by Vishnu's Narasimha incarnation, and Taraka, a powerful demon vanquished by Shiva, are other examples. There are many more such legends in Hinduism. The Rigveda mentions the word "asura" more than 80 times, while describing beings with varied characteristics. And despite them being classified into diverse groups, asura is the name given to most Hindu demons. These beings are as powerful as gods and sometimes even overshadow them in several legends. Some groups of asuras or power-seeking demon clans related to the more benevolent devas have also been added to the Hindu pantheon.

The asuras constantly battle the gods. Sometimes, these beings possess excellent qualities, such as wisdom, intelligence, strength and courage. Despite their often evil roles, some asuras are depicted as complex characters with admirable traits, but for the most part, they are sinful. The range of asuras in Hinduism include rakshasa, pishachas, danavas, daityas and yakshas. Out of these different types, the main groups of demons are rakshasas, who are always shown fighting the devas. Rakshasas are depicted in various forms, including human, animal, half-human and half-animal. They sometimes have multiple heads, large or many arms, and numerous eyes. At times, some of them have four legs and only one eye. They can become enormous, with prominent, long and sharp teeth, and multiple hands and heads. In several scriptures, these rakshasas are portrayed as, quite plainly, monsters.

Interestingly, the Bhagavad Gita says that the world and human beings have both essences; some possess Daviya Sampada or divine cult, and others have Asura Sampada or sinister cult.

These demons are generally respected but not worshiped in the same manner as gods. Instead, they are mainly revered by small communities in villages who sometimes build temples to honor them. These shrines are often simple structures or just sacred trees where people offer rituals to seek blessings from the asuras. While no elaborate yagnas or mantras are recited, offerings are made to appease them.

RAVANA
The Legendary Emperor of Lanka

Ravana, the great demon king of Lanka, was the antagonist of the epic, Ramayana. His life's greatest sin was abducting Sita and bringing her to his kingdom. According to ancient Hindu scriptures, Ravana was born to a rakshasi princess, Kaikesi. He was the great-grandson of Brahma and son to rishi Vishrava. Ravana's wife Mandodari was the daughter of the architect Maya, and their mighty son, Meghanada, had even defeated Indra in a war. Though a feared demon, Ravana was a learned scholar, well-versed in the six shastras and a master of the four Vedas. In fact, Ravana's teacher was Shukracharya, the guru of the asuras.

Furthermore, Ravana had many brothers and sisters. One of the most well-known brothers was Kumbhakarna, who used to sleep for six months in a year and then stay awake for the next six. According to the Bhagavata Purana, Ravana and Kumbhakarna were said to be the reincarnations of Jaya and Vijaya, the gatekeepers at Vaikuntha, the abode of Vishnu. They were cursed by the sages Sanaka, Sanandana, Sanatana and Sanatkumara. The sages, also known as Manasaputras, were created from the mind of Brahma and represent the embodiment of thought and intellect. They cursed the gatekeepers to reincarnate on Earth as demon kings. In some of the Puranas, Ravana is depicted with 10 heads. But mostly, he is shown with nine heads only, as he cut one off as an offering to Shiva. The Lanka king had exceptional weapons, including a chariot that could fly, which he had seized from Kubera.

If Hindu legends are to be believed, Ravana's kingdom Lanka is the modern-day Sri Lanka. He ruled there with his mighty powers over humans, gods and other demons. Contrary to his depictions in most of India, in Sri Lanka, Ravana is portrayed as a great ruler, scholar and legendary king. In fact, Lanka is believed to have prospered under his rule. Ravana was a scientist and his contribution to the fields of Ayurveda, Tantra and astrology are significant. He researched Atharvademuklaya, and developed the Indrajaal and Arka Prakasha. He even had physicians in his court like Sushena, who knew everything about life-saving drugs—their location, qualities and religious significance—found in his country as well as foreign lands.

In the Valmiki Ramayana, Ravana kidnapped Rama's wife, Sita, as Rama and his brother, Lakshmana, had sliced off his sister, Surpanakha's nose. Eventually, in the battle between Rama and Ravana, the demon king was killed and Sita was rescued. In Sri Lanka, though, there is a different version which adds that Vibhishana, one of Ravana's brothers, wanted to become the king. Therefore, he helped Rama, who managed to cross the waters to reach Lanka and defeat the world's most remarkable ruler, Ravana. This version also states that it was on the orders of Ravana that with the help of Sushena Vaidya, an unconscious Lakshmana's life was saved using the Sanjeevani herb. In fact, the human-made landmass bridge, Rama-Setu, which Rama's army used to cross the sea and get to Sri Lanka, was built by Ravana, as per Lankan religious lore. Incidentally, Sri Lanka named its first satellite, Raavana 1, after the king.

The most reverant devotee of Shiva, Ravana performed severe penance to appease the god for several hundred years. At the end of the ritual, Ravana chopped off his head many times to get Shiva's blessings. Whenever he cut off his head, though, a new one emerged with the grace of Shiva. Eventually, the god was impressed with Ravana's sacrifice and austerity, and offered him a boon. Ravana wanted to be immortal, a power Shiva refused to grant. Shiva, instead, gifted Ravana the nectar of immortality, which the demon king had to stow under his navel—till the time the nectar was tucked safely there, no harm could come to Ravana. In another tale, Ravana decided to bring Mount Kailash to Lanka for his mother. He managed to lift the entire mountain, but Shiva got angry and pushed him down. Hence, to please Shiva, Ravana created a new musical instrument using his body parts and chanted the *Shiva Tandava Stotram*. This musical instrument is known as the Ravanhatha today. Hearing the harmony produced by the stotram and the musical instrument, coupled with Ravana's fierce dedication, Shiva was immensely gratified. He cried tears of joy and forgave Ravana. The Shiva Tandava Stotram is one of the well-known hymns of Shiva and is intoned widely.

Despite being a demon, Ravana is still venerated in some places of India. In the Bisrakh village of Uttar Pradesh, in the area known as Greater Noida, not only is Ravana worshiped, but in a marked departure from the customs followed in most of India, his effigy is not burned on Dussehra. This is because Bisrakh is believed by some to be the birthplace of Ravana. Similarly, in Jodhpur, Rajasthan, there is a famous Ravana temple, where the demon king is worshiped as the chief deity. There are also some temples of Shiva where Ravana is venerated along with the god as his most devout disciple. Furthermore, there are many temples of Ravana in Sri Lanka, where he is praised and revered.

LORD KUBERA
The God of Wealth

Kubera is the treasurer of the gods. The god of wealth is a demigod from the yaksha community, which is similar to the asuras. Yakshas, however, are portrayed as helpful supernatural beings.

Interestingly, the meaning of Kubera in Sanskrit is "deformed or ill-shaped." He is often portrayed as a big-bellied dwarf with a fair complexion, golden clothes and lots of ornaments. Kubera recieved his mace from Vishwakarma: the weapon was fashioned from Surya's powers when Vishwakarma sliced off some of the sun god's brilliance in an effort to to help him live with his wife. At times, Kubera is also depicted with a single eye, three legs and many teeth. He was the half-brother of Ravana, one of the most legendary asuras. Kubera's wife is Bhadra, a Yakshi. She is the daughter of the demon Mura. Despite his lineage, Kubera gains the status of a deva in the Puranas and other Hindu epics. Additionally, he is considered the wealthiest among the gods.

According to some legends, Kubera's father Rishi Vishrava, married a rakshasi princess, Kaikesi, whose four other children are Ravana, Kumbhakarna, Vibhishana and Surpanakha. After getting a boon from Brahma and becoming tremendously powerful, Ravana usurped the Lanka throne, seized the palace and took away Kubera's Pushpaka Vimana. Kubera was the king of Lanka and he had built the palace with the help of Vishwakarma; the magnificence of the court is described in the Mahabharata and the Puranas. In the ensuing conflict between the half-brothers, most demons backed Ravana. After losing his kingdom and his home, Kubera moved to Gandhamanda Mountain near Mount Kailash, Shiva's abode. Later, because of the long periods of austerity observed by him, he received a boon from Brahma, and with that the god of wealth was able to restore his status.

In a well-known tale, Kubera had lent money to Venkateshwara (also known as Srinivasa), one of the manifestations of Vishnu, for his upcoming nuptials with Padmavati. Padmavati was a princess, but Venkateshwara had been incarnated as a poor man. To cover the wedding expenses, Venkateshwara borrowed money from Kubera and promised to repay the loan, with interest, before the Kali Yuga ended. Till this day, many devotees at the Tirupati temple donate money to Venkateshwara's pot to help him pay back Kubera. All the donations made by Venkateshwara's devotees are considered as the interest accrued on the loan from Kubera. Another form of contribution, particular to this temple, is when a devotee gives up their possessions—including money and jewelry— and goes back empty-handed and penniless. Devotees repay the god's loan in the hope that he will do the same for them. If the devotees try to cheat in terms of the promises made or attempt to pinch pennies, the god recovers the interest in the form of a punishment. Despite all this, Kubera does not hold an indispensable position in Hinduism like Lakshmi. However, numerous tales abound of him lending money to other gods.

Sometimes Lakshmi is worshiped along with Kubera as Shri Lakshmi Kubera. There are very few independent Kubera temples in India but there are various mantras dedicated to him. It is believed that by chanting these mantras, one is blessed with wealth and success. Sometimes people keep the Kubera idol or yantra at home. During Diwali, on the day of Dhantrayodashi, also known as Dhanteras, Kubera is worshiped alongside Lakshmi and Ganesha. The purchase of gold on this day is considered auspicious. Another important day for Kubera is Sharad Purnima, his birthday. Offerings and prayers to Kubera on this day hold immense significance.

In some parts of India, Kubera is regarded as a Vedic deity, while Lakshmi is considered to a Puranic deity. In some texts, Kubera is the keeper of wealth, whereas Lakshmi distributes wealth and prosperity. Kubera is not only popular in the Hindu pantheon but is a prominent god in Buddhism and Jainism as well. In the former, he is Vaisravana and in the latter, Jambhala—again, as the one who protects dharma and is the god of wealth. Inspite of his associations with wealth and prosperity in Hinduism, Kubera gets overshadowed by Ganesha.

MAHABALI
The Daitya King

Mahabali, also known as Bali, was king of the daityas, according to Hindu scriptures. Unlike other asuras, he never committed any atrocities. He was a devoted follower of Vishnu: being the grandson of Prahlada the strong foundations of his devotion to the god had been laid out since childhood. Mahabali had many good qualities. He was charitable, and he respected gods, priests and sages.

As per Vishnu Purana, when Mahabali became the king of daityas, he commenced a war with the gods to become the ruler of all three worlds. Soon after, he defeated Indra and the other devas, and almost succeeded in ruling over all three realms. Following their defeat, the devas approached Vishnu for help. However, he refused to join the gods against Mahabali because the daitya was an exceptional ruler and a faithful devotee. Later, Mahabali decided to perform a yagna known as the Ashwamedha Yagna, the fulfillment of which would have made him the king of all three worlds. In an attempt to stop the yagna, Vishnu finally decided to intervene, and hence was incarnated as the Vamana avatar. This avatar, a poor Brahmin boy, attended the yagna and asked Bali for a measure of land that could be covered in three footsteps. Despite warnings from Guru Shukracharya that the Vamana was Vishnu himself, and therefore, Bali shouldn't accede to his request, the king agreed to grant him the land. Soon after, the Vamana became gigantic in size. His first step covered the entire Earth and the underworld. In the second step, he took the Svarga and sky. Then, the Brahmin boy asked where he should put his next and last step. Seeing that, the daitya king offered him his head. Vishnu was pleased with the level of Bali's devotion—he gave Mahabali a boon, ensuring that despite losing all his possessions, he would be loved by Vishnu and his followers. He was also promised a high-ranking position in Vaikuntha.

The festival Onam is a tribute to the sacrifice of King Mahabali. Onam is the harvest festival that falls in the months of August/September. It is celebrated across India and the world, but it is the main festival among the people of Kerala, India. It is believed that King Mahabali still visits his people in this state on the second day of the Onam festival.

ANCESTORS TO BENEFICENT GUARDIAN SPIRITS

Ancestor worship has been an integral part of Hindu tradition, dating back to the early Vedic times. People have been performing these rituals and making offering to ancestors for many millennia now. In Hinduism, immediately after the demise of a person, the last ritual, called Antyeshti Sanskara, is performed to pay tribute to the departed soul. There are altogether 16 sanskaras through the course of one's life. It starts from the Garbhadhan, which is at the child's conception, and ends in Antyeshti Sanskara. After the Antyeshti is completed, the atman or soul permanently separates from the deceased body and leaves the physical world. The atman and the body share a profound connection throughout a person's life. Once the material body has fulfilled its purpose, it can no longer sustain life, necessitating the atman's departure and transition to the next stage of existence. This transition is commonly known as reincarnation or rebirth. Karma significantly influences the atman's subsequent life and experiences. The ultimate goal, however, is moksha—the liberation of the atman from the endless cycle of birth and death.

Cremation is the most common method of conducting a funeral ceremony in Hinduism. However, certain groups and castes do not cremate their dead; instead they bury the body. Ascetics and children are generally buried or cast into water bodies with flowing water. In Hinduism, the body and atman are always two independent entities, and even if the body dies, the atman continues to exist.

Spiritual Body and Soul

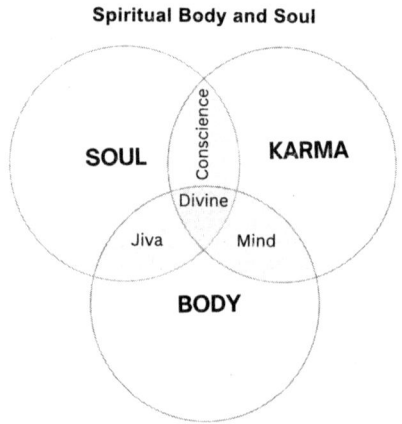

Ancient scriptures state that once the soul separates from the deceased's body, it is often reluctant to leave, as material desires keep it attached to the corpse. Furthermore, the soul is distressed to see the family and friends in agony. The soul's connection to the world, through the body, makes it reluctant to leave. After the deceased's body is cremated, the last sanskara cuts off the soul's attachment to the physical body. Agni, in the ultimate rite, returns the body to the five elements of its origin. The body is reduced to five tatvas or elements. In Hinduism, everything in the universe, including the human body, comprises Panchtatvas or five elements. These Panchtatvas connote the following: akash or sky, vayu or wind, agni or fire, jal or water and prithvi or earth. The scriptures that describe funereal ceremonies in detail are the Atharvaveda, the Aranyaka of Krishna Yajurveda and the Sutras.

At the funeral, the family and friends take the deceased's body to the cremation area. The cremation ground is purified, and the fire is lit with logs of wood and ghee, a type of clarified butter. Mantras are recited and the body is offered to the fire—this becomes the physical body's final purification rite. During the post-death rituals, the family of the deceased makes donations or does charity work on the departed person's behalf. This helps the soul in its journey in the afterlife. Thereafter, even when the soul leaves the body, it retains some connection with the physical world for the next 13 days. All the final ceremonies related to cremation and mourning are completed within these days. The rituals not only help guide the soul to moksha but also provide solace to the deceased's family.

In the days following the death, Hindus recite hymns from the Garuda Purana, along with other prayers to help the soul reach its final destination. When the atman leaves the body, it adopts another spiritual form. This form grows slowly, day by day. On the tenth day after the death, the form grows to its fullest capacity, and the family of the deceased offers pindas or food balls made of rice and water, to help prepare the soul for the next life. During this period, the soul is called "pret," something that has not reached the next world yet. On the eleventh day, prayers are performed for the soul to witness Vishnu and Yama. On the twelfth and thirteenth day, the soul reaches the next world and resides with the family's ancestors called "pitra," and the Antyeshti is considered complete. After that, every year, the family performs rituals on a fixed day in a specific month, for the deceased. The ritual is called shradh, which is a symbol of remembrance and respect. Shradh is a Sanskrit word that means "to perform with sincere faith and respect." On this day, the memory of the deceased is evoked. It is performed in the Pitra-Paksha as per the Bikram Sambat Hindu calendar. Some of the rituals are performed either by the eldest son or the youngest. The shradh can be performed for fathers, mothers, step-parents, grandparents, great-grandparents—both paternal and maternal. It can also be performed for wives, children, brothers, sisters, uncles, aunts, cousins, in-laws, and one's guru. According to the Puranas, every Hindu, whoever has the means, should partake in charity for the poor during Pitra-Paksha. We owe our existence to our ancestors. Hence, they are equivalent to gods in Hinduism.

On the day of the ritual, it is important to invite priests so that they can offer food to the deceased. Sometimes, even a yagna is performed for the ancestors with additional prayers and offerings for the entire community of pitra. It should be accomplished on the Tithi or the death anniversary as per the

Hindu calendar. Soon after the Pitra-Paksha, the Navaratri festival starts, followed by Diwali.

The shradh is one of the most critical and noble rituals in the Hindu religion. It expresses one's unconditional love, faith and reverence. According to the ancient texts, this offering is a debt on every individual that must be fulfilled by performing acts of charity. It is said that those who manage to do the ritual, depending on their capability and faith, get blessings from ancestors for themselves and the family. It is believed that petra/pitra, the beneficent guardian spirit, protects the family from evil.

NATURE AND
CELESTIAL
BODIES

Hinduism is a unique religion that deeply integrates the spiritual with the natural world. Nature worship is a significant aspect of Hinduism. Hindus believe that the divine is present in all aspects of nature, from the smallest creatures to the vast cosmos. Therefore, gods can exist in all manner of beings created by nature, whether they be animals, mountains, trees, rivers or the celestial bodies, to name a few examples. This belief fosters a deep sense of respect, reverence and care toward the environment and underscores the significant role of nature in the spiritual and cultural fabric of the religion.

An example that illustrates this principle is that of the Ganga River, which possesses immense importance in Hindu rituals. Bathing in its waters purifies and grants salvation to those who lead righteous lives. Every year, millions of people are cremated along the banks of the Ganga.

Similarly, the paradigm of diverse worship in Hinduism includes the Kalpavriksha tree and Kamadhenu, the divine cow, beings that emerged from the Samudra Manthan. Ancient scriptures and texts like the Vedas, the Mahabharata, the Bhagavad Gita and the Puranas talk about the importance of trees and preserving nature. Likewise, the cow has been considered a sacred animal since the Vedic age.

Celestial bodies such as the sun and moon are also revered as Vedic deities, known as Surya and Chandra, respectively. Additionally, the five planets—Budha or Mercury, Shukra or Venus, Mangala or Mars, Brihaspati or Jupiter and Shani or Saturn—have significant status in Hinduism. These celestial bodies are also associated with days of the week in the Hindu calendar and are believed to greatly influence a Hindu person's life. Even in present-day Hinduism, these planets receive offerings during primary festivals like Diwali and Dussehra. Hindu rituals always involve honoring these heavenly bodies. These varied practices showcase how Hinduism weaves spiritual beliefs together, honoring both nature and the cosmic elements as integral parts of its cultural heritage.

GOD'S CREATIONS:
HOLY TREES AND PLANTS

Hinduism is deeply integrated with all the forms of nature. Nearly all the ancient temples in India have sacred trees on their premises. A tree in a temple is generally called Sthala Vriksha. The worship of plants and trees is one of the oldest forms of worship in Hinduism. Mother Earth, the primitive deity has been worshiped since the early Vedic age. The worship of trees, plants and vegetation has played a vital role in the religion. Different trees, plants, herbs and shrubs are revered as a holistic part of God, or in some other divine form. Plants and flowers are also used in decorations for temples, in Hindu marriages, and major or minor festivals. Interestingly, even zodiac signs in Hinduism are associated with various trees.

Therefore, worshiping trees has been a longstanding tradition in Hinduism. Sacred trees have different names in ancient scriptures, like Kalpavriksha or Chaityavriksha. Kalpavriksha means "the tree of life" or "the world tree." The Kalpavriksha emerged during the churning of the cosmic ocean, the Samudra Manthan. The title Kalpavriksha is primarily associated with the banyan tree. Whereas Chaityavriksha refers to umbrella-like trees that provide shelter to human beings, birds and animals. According to the Matsya Purana, planting a tree is equivalent to the good deeds of 10 sons:

दशकूपसमा वापी, दशवापीसमो हृदः।
दशहृदसमो पुत्रो, दशपुत्रसमो द्रुमः!

Dashkupsama wapi, dashwapisamo hradah,
Dashhradasmo putro, dashputrasamo drumah.

Translation

A pond equals 10 wells, and a reservoir equals 10 ponds.
A son equals 10 reservoirs, and a tree equals 10 sons!

—*Matsaya Purana*

The Aryans of the early Vedic period were pantheists and worshipers of nature. The Rigveda considers Soma to be an essential plant. An entire chapter in the it, called the Soma Mandala, talks about the rituals of purifying Soma. Soma was the drink of that period, produced from a special type of plant. Besides Soma, the Rigveda talks about pipal, bamboo and other sacred trees. It also mentions the rituals related to grass, flowers and leaves.

The Ramayana references sacred plants and trees like tulsi, pipal, banyan and banana. For instance, in Lanka, Sita was confined under the sacred ashoka tree. There was also the badari tree, which assisted Rama when he was searching for Sita in the Panchavati forest.

The Mahabharata also discusses the significance of trees on many occasions. Kadamba is designated as Krishna's favorite tree. The Vrindavan forests are mentioned in the epic as well: this tells us about Krishna's affection for trees and Mother Nature. Similarly, in the Puranas, like the Matsya Purana, Padma Purana and Narasimha Purana, numerous stories revolve around trees or plants and the rituals associated with their worship.

Some of the most sacred trees and plants in Hinduism are:

Pipal Tree: The pipal tree is revered in the Hindu sacred texts, symbolizing Brahma, Vishnu and Shiva; its roots are seen as Brahma, the trunk as Vishnu and the leaves as Shiva. Worshiped primarily on Saturdays, it is believed to protect one from diseases and enemies. Those who worship the pipal tree on this day are said to receive blessings from Lakshmi. It is common to see red threads or pieces of cloth tied around the branches of these trees across India. Pipal trees are frequently found in the temples of Vishnu, Hanuman and Shani as well.

In the Hindu tradition, parikrama or circumambulating the pipal tree is considered auspicious because the act supposedly grants blessings and fulfills wishes. Watering the pipal tree is believed to bring goodwill not only to oneself but also to future generations.

Banyan Tree: This tree is considered sacred because of Vishnu. It symbolizes immortality. Generally, banyan trees are found near temples. But it is not unusual for a shrine to exist under the tree, either. The Sanskrit name of the tree is Nyagrodha, which means "the down-grower." Once planted, this tree grows and propagates itself by striking its branches into the soil through hanging tendrils, which take root. Hence, the tree keeps growing for centuries. Kabirvad is a banyan tree on a small river island near the Narmada River, in Gujarat, India. This place and the tree are linked to the fifteenth-century mystic poet, Kabir. The banyan tree is also the national tree of India. No other tree has as many folklore and mythological stories associated with it. The banyan tree is also called Vat or Bargad in Hindi.

This tree can grow and survive for centuries and is distinguished for being able to provide shelter to its devotees. Its large leaves are frequently used for worshiping and performing rituals. Sometimes the banyan is associated with Yama too. This is why it is found outside of village boundaries, near crematoriums. Also, owing to its medicinal and healing characteristics, it is used widely in Ayurveda.

Tulsi Plant: The basil or tulsi plant is probably the most cultivated and holiest plant in Hinduism. As per Hindu beliefs, this sacred plant represents Tulsi, an incarnation of Lakshmi. Basil leaves are widely used in herbal teas and Ayurvedic medicines and are also added to all food prepared for every Hindu god. In most temples, these leaves are given as part of prasada or sacred food offerings in temples. The tulsi plant is a small shrub with small red, green or purple leaves. It has a pleasing aroma. Tulsi is an important home plant for many Hindu families. It is planted in unique pot structures known as Tulsi Vrindavan. The plant is usually placed in the center of the courtyard or balcony.

Tulsi, too, has many stories associated with it. Once, a woman named Tulsi wanted to marry Vishnu. But she was the daughter of Kalanemi, an asura. She performed a long penance and eventually, Vishnu was impressed. He assured her that she could wed one of his incarnations, which was Shaligram. Thereafter, Vishnu came to Earth in the form of the Shaligram stone and married Tulsi. Tulsi Vivah is still celebrated in many parts of India. It is observed as a formal wedding as per traditional Hindu wedding rituals. Tulsi is also an integral part of Krishna's worship. Garlands made of 1,000 tulsi leaves, water mixed with tulsi and food items sprinkled with tulsi are offered to Vishnu and Krishna. In the Vaishnava tradition, a tulsi mala or prayer beads is used for japa or prayer. In fact, the Padma Purana says if a person is cremated with tulsi twigs in their mouth, their soul is bound to achieve moksha. The soul finds its place in Vishnu's abode, Vaikuntha Dham. On the other hand, sometimes it is discouraged to worship Shiva with tulsi leaves, but this is not mentioned in the Puranas or other ancient scriptures.

Apart from these, many other sacred trees, plants and flowers are honored in Hinduism as well. For instance, bael is associated with the worship of Shiva. Leaves of bael are laid on shivalinga to cool the deity. It is believed that even if a devotee only offers bael leaves and water, Shiva accepts it with grace. In fact, his worship is deemed incomplete without these leaves. However, the fruits of the bael tree are not offered to him. Another important tree is neem—it is included in the worship of the tutelary goddess Shitala Mata, a smallpox deity, as neem leaves are known for their healing and medicinal properties. Other sacred trees are banana, ashoka, mango, coconut and mulberry. One of India's oldest sacred trees, famously known as the Kalpavriksha, is located at Joshimath, Uttarakhand. This mulberry tree is believed to be 1,200 years old. It is said that Adi Shankaracharya sat under this tree and paid homage to Shiva. The shivalinga created by him still exists in the Jyoteshwar Mahadev Temple built under this tree.

Since the Vedic period, Kusha, a specific type of grass, is prominently used in yagnas. Among flowers, lotus is oft mentioned in the Puranas. This sacred flower is associated with Lakshmi and Vishnu. Also, Brahma was born from a lotus, which sprung from Vishnu's navel, as per some mythological stories. Each god in Hinduism is associated with one or the other type of flower, leaf, tree or plant, thus clearly depicting the religion's strong connection with nature.

Another example is the Rudraksha, which is a seed of the *Elaeocarpus ganitrus* tree, and is used to make prayer beads for Shiva. The beads are commonly worn for protection or while chanting mantras. In Sanskrit, "raksha" means "to protect." This tree is mainly found at the foothills of the Himalayas in India, Nepal and South Asia and Southeast Asia.

SACRED RIVERS AND LAKES

The sacred Ganga is worshiped as a goddess in Hindu mythology, sacred texts and scriptures. Some of the most important and the oldest cities of the world such as Prayag (Allahabad, or Prayagraj as it is now known as), Patliputra (Patna) and Kasi (Varanasi) are situated on its banks. The Ganga originated from the Gangotri glacier called Gaumukh, which means "mouth of the cow." This sacred river has held a place of importance in Hinduism since centuries. The river's water has witnessed the lives of Rama, Krishna, Buddha and many other ancient seers and immortals. Although, it is the Saraswati that was considered the most holy in the Rigveda, that river dried up many centuries ago. And so, in medieval times and the present-day, the Ganga is considered the most sacred river on Earth. It not only descended from Svarga but is also a doorway to Heaven for humans. The river water is pure; it forgives one's sins. One of the standard religious practices of Hinduism is taking a bath on the banks of the Ganga. Many festivals are organized every year, in which millions of Hindus bathe on the banks of this sacred river. One such religious gathering is the Maha Kumbh Mela, one of the largest religious festivals in the world that is held in one place.

Ganga holds an important place in the Hindu pantheon—she is the daughter of Himavan. Her younger sister was Parvati, the wife of Shiva. Ganga is generally represented as a fair-complexioned woman, wearing a white crown, often sitting on a crocodile with a lily in her right hand and a flute in her left. Sometimes, she is also depicted with four arms, carrying a small pot or jar, with her other hands in the Abhaya Mudra.

Numerous legends recount how Ganga came down to Earth. One among these many stories mention that once, there was a war between devas and asuras. When the devas won, for many years, the asuras tried to hide from them and went deep inside the Kshirasagara ocean. The gods were unable to locate them. The great seer Agastya finally found the demons, but he had to drink the seawater to expose their hiding place. As the asuras' hiding spot was revealed, they were slayed by Indra. But there was also no more water left on Earth. Everyone prayed to Indra, who declared that a river would flow from Heaven to the earthly realms if Shiva was worshiped instead.

In another tale, a king named Sagara, in an effort to establish his strength as a ruler, decided to perform an Ashwamedha Yagna. This yagna required a horse to be sent across the world. Unfortunately, the asuras captured the animal and hid it away. The mighty King Sagara dispatched his 60,000 sons, offspring he had magically acquired, to find the horse. Eventually, they found the horse near the sage Kapila's hut. The arrogant sons deemed the powerful ascetic to be the thief and awoke him from his meditation. Enraged at being disrespected and having had his penance disrupted, Kapila opened his eyes and reduced Sagara's sons to ashes.

After several years, Sagara's grandsons found the ashes to perform the funeral ceremonies for their fathers. They needed sacred water for the rites. King Sagara and his grandsons tried to appeal to the holy river to descend from Heaven but their efforts were in vain. Several grandsons tried to demonstrate their devotion and perform severe austerities, but they remained unsuccessful. At long last, Bhagiratha, one of King Sagara's great-grandchildren, performed a strict penance to please Shiva. Impressed, Shiva let a small stream of the Ganga flow from his head, which descended from the Himalayas to the land below. Shiva controlled the flow as the entirety of the river would have swept away the whole planet. Similarly, there are many other interesting stories about Ganga in the Mahabharata. She is worshiped across India in many temples. A part of the Char Dham temples, the Gangotri is worth visiting at least once in a lifetime. Situated at 10,200 feet, in a rarefied atmosphere, it seems to exude divinity—and it also happens to be the place where Bhagiratha supposedly performed the penance that brought forth Ganga to Earth.

Few things are more remarkable in today's world than the sight of countless devotees at one of the Varanasi ghats swarming into the sacred river to cleanse their souls, or just watching the vibrant Ganga Aarti held along the serene beauty of the calm, holy river.

Along with Ganga, Saraswati was one of the principal goddesses in the Vedic period. In fact, the goddess of knowledge, Saraswati, is mentioned in the Rigveda numerous times as the personification of the river. However, it is believed that this river dried up a long time ago. The Brahmaputra is another essential river and is also considered a deity. The second-largest tributary of the Ganga, the Yamuna is another sacred river. Also known as Yami, Yamuna is Yama's sister and Surya's daughter. There are many religious beliefs associated with the Yamuna that happen to involve Krishna too. Various such stories are mentioned in the Puranas. Other than that, the rivers, Godavari and Kaveri, are worshiped as well. Since the days of the Indus Valley civilization, river worship has been prominent in Hinduism, reflecting the religion's connection to the various phases and aspects of life, from birth to death.

In Hinduism, certain lakes and ponds are also considered holy. There are five sacred lakes, collectively called the Panch Sarovar. These are Mansarovar, Bindu Sarovar, Narayan Sarovar, Pampa Sarovar and Pushkar Sarovar.

One of the highest freshwater lakes in the world, Mansarovar is located in present-day China, nestled amid the Kailash glaciers. The holy Pushkar Sarovar is in the town of Pushkar in Ajmer, Rajasthan. This lake is associated with the tales of Brahma. It has around 52 bathing ghats, where many pilgrims cleanse themselves as it is believed to cure skin diseases. As per the Puranas, it was first created in Brahma's mind, after which it manifested on Earth. Bindu Sarovar, located in Siddhapur, Gujarat, is said to be the universe's first source of water. Bathing in it is believed to cleanse one's sins. Narayan Sarovar, in Kutch, Gujarat, is considered to be Vishnu's abode. Sacred to Vaishnava devotees, a dip in it is said to grant salvation. Near Hampi, Karnataka, Pampa Sarovar is where Parvati performed penance to win Shiva—taking a plunge in it is believed to bestow marital fidelity, making it holy for Shiva devotees. Apart from this, many other lakes are also worshiped by specific sects of the Hindu religion across India, so much so that these water bodies are only revered by the people native to that particular region.

DEVOTION TOWARD ANIMALS AND BIRDS

In Hinduism, several animals are also linked to the gods, and they too are occasionally worshiped. It is believed that animals have a soul just like humans, and when they die, they can also reincarnate as a human or an animal again. Nevertheless, not all animals are deemed sacred. One of the primary reasons some are considered divine is because they are the vahana of the Hindu gods. Gods use rats, tigers, elephants, bulls, snakes, and many more such animals to travel. But these animals also represent their power. They are even mentioned in the Rigveda.

Animal exploitation is discouraged in all the Hindu religious scriptures. Yet in ancient times, in certain communities and sects, animal sacrifices were performed during the rituals of worship for certain gods. However, Hinduism is the only religion where all life forms, including plants, animals and fishes are worshiped and honored. The respect for animal rights has been derived from the doctrine of ahimsa or nonviolence, spiritual purity, and to an extent, from vegetarianism. Hinduism has a strong association with vegetarianism, though it's not a universal requirement and not a mandatory practice. It is more accurate to say that vegetarianism is a widely practiced and valued tradition within Hinduism, influenced by various factors such as religious beliefs, cultural practices and personal preferences.

In modern Hinduism, too, certain animals are said to possess religious and symbolic value. They are associated with different gods, like monkeys who are linked with Hanuman, elephants and rats with Ganesha, and tigers with Durga. But none other is as revered as the cow. However, it is also important to understand that no animal, including the cow, is recognized as a god in Hinduism. They are sacred symbols of Hinduism that are protected, revered and associated with Hindu gods.

Cow: The concept of cow protection in modern times is imperative for various reasons. The animal is referred to as a mother and symbolizes Earth. Indra's Kamadhenu cow arose during the cosmic ocean's churning and could fulfill any wishes. Kamadhenu, also known as Surabhi, is the symbolic mother of all cows.

According to the Mahabharata, Kamadhenu emerged from the churning of the cosmic ocean and was given to the Saptarishi. She was instructed to provide milk so that ghee could be used for rituals during Agni Yagnas. However, it is rare to find a temple dedicated solely to Kamadhenu. For Vaishnava sects, the cow is an embodiment of Lakshmi. In the Bhagavata Purana, Earth is symbolized as a cow, whose guardian is Vishnu. The cow appears in numerous legends, with representations that vary across stories. Among the many mythological stories associated with it are tales that feature Krishna in a major way. Krishna grew up as a cow herder; his other names include Govinda or Gopala, which mean "friend or protector of the cow." Gopashtami is a festival that reveres Krishna and cows—on this day, devotees visit the goshala or cow shelter and feed the cows, and both Krishna and the animals are worshiped during the puja. According to the Vedas, the cow encompasses all the gods and goddesses, including the Trinity, and also acts as an abode for them. In Hinduism, it is highly auspicious to feed a cow. Consequently, the biggest sin is to kill a cow or eat its meat.

Snake: The snake is another animal with a high status in the religion's ancient scriptures. It is known as "naga" in Sanskrit. Many legends in the Puranas involve tales of snakes. Naag Panchami, a festival of great significance, is associated with snake worship. On this day, snake idols are offered milk in rural India. Hinduism has many legends that tell the stories of snakes like Shesh Naga, Vasuki Naga and more. Snakes are also closely associated with Shiva, who is frequently depicted with a snake coiled around his neck. In yogic traditions, the snake symbolizes kundalini energy, which represents a dormant spiritual power situated at the base of the spine.

Monkey: Monkeys are revered as sacred creatures, closely associated with the beloved deity Hanuman. Often seen as symbols of devotion and loyalty, they are considered his pious companions. This deep reverence is reflected in numerous temples across India where thousands of monkeys roam freely.

Devotees frequently visit these sacred sites, offering food and prayers as a form of worship, believing that by caring for these monkeys, they honor Hanuman himself. The lively presence of these animals not only enhances the spiritual atmosphere, but also creates a vibrant connection between the divine and the natural world, inviting visitors to experience a unique blend of devotion and joy.

Garuda: Garuda is a half-human and half-bird creature, with an eagle's head and wings. He is worshiped together with Vishnu, and is viewed as the king of all birds. This being is the son of Kashyapa, a sage, and Vinata, King Daksha's daughter. There are several mythological stories about Garuda in the Puranas and other scriptures.

SACRED STONES

Sacred stones hold immense significance in Hinduism and are revered and worshiped as powerful symbols of divine presence. They embody cosmic energies and serve as profound conduits for devotion, meditation and spiritual connection for believers. One such unique stone is the shaligram. Scientifically, shaligrams may be black-colored fossilized stones that are the remains of extinct sea-dwelling ammonites, but to the devotees of Vishnu, the specific shape, markings and color of the stone represent the various forms and aspects of the god. The Vishnu Purana and the Skanda Purana specifically mention shaligrams, describing them as sacred stones that represent Vishnu. This stone represents an abstract symbolism pertaining to this god. Shaligrams are habitually found in riverbeds, especially on the banks of the Gandaki River in present-day Nepal. They have fossil marks on the inside that are considered to be the chakra of Vishnu. These stones are worshiped for gaining wisdom, good virtues, courage and success in all endeavors. Shaligrams are sacred because they are not human-made, and the geological formation processes imbibe them with a living essence of their own. They are worshiped in both temples and homes as manifestations of the divine.

According to the Varaha Purana, Salankayana, a descendant of the eminent sage Vishwamitra, wanted a secluded place to perform severe austerities. His aim was to attain a glimpse of Vishnu. After a long journey, he arrived at the banks of the Gandaki. Finding a suitable spot beneath a shaala tree, Salankayana began his rigorous penance. His devotion and perseverance over countless years, moved Vishnu, who finally appeared before the sage, offering to bestow any boon upon him. Salankayana, however, only desired to see the god in his divine form. Pleased with the sage's humility, Vishnu granted Salankayana's wish and manifested his divine form before him.

From that day forward, the site where Salankayana performed his penance became known as Shaligram Tirtha, a revered pilgrimage destination. It is located near the Gandak River in Nepal, specifically in the Myagdi district. This sacred site is close to the town of Beni, which serves as a gateway for pilgrims visiting the area. The Shaligram stones found in the area, from the Gandaki Riverbed, are considered manifestations of Vishnu. Hindus believe worshiping a Shaligram stone can bestow blessings, spiritual growth and offer protection. This sacred connection has made the Shaligram Tirtha an important site for devotees seeking divine favor.

NAVAGRAHA
The Nine Heavenly Bodies

Since ancient times, it has been assumed that celestial bodies can influence and shape our destinies. In Hinduism, astrology is the science of stars, which predicts future events with the help of a birth chart or horoscope. A birth chart or horoscope is the pictorial representation of the placement of stars and planets at the time of a person's birth on a particular date, time and place. In this chart, critical factors are considered, which are the building blocks of a person's life. Major aspects of the horoscope include:

- Solar system
- Zodiac sign
- Planets
- Nakshatras
- Time and place of birth

Among these, the Navagraha—the nine celestial bodies—have a central place in Hindu scriptures and astrology.

"Nava" means "nine," and "graha" means "the planet." As per Hindu astrology, this collective cosmic mass influences the life of human beings on Earth. Graha are the planets of our solar system. Different mythological stories about the Navagraha can be found in the epics and in the Puranas, like Brahmanda Purana, Matsya Purana, Shiva Purana, Linga Purana, Kurma Garuda, Vayu Purana and Bhavishya Purana. Interestingly, Valmiki had mentioned the planetary positions at the time of Rama's birth. Similarly, during Mahabharata, the possible dates for critical events and wars were provided using the Navagraha. The Navagraha are studied as a principal subject in Hinduism, and play a significant role in deciding the destiny of individuals.

Hindus worship all nine heavenly bodies, out of which two are the corresponding Vedic gods, namely, Surya and Chandra. Apart from these two, there are five other planets—Budha, Shukra, Mangala, Brihaspati and Shani. The remaining are the north and south shadow of the lunar node called Rahu and Ketu. Sometimes, Shani, Rahu and Ketu are considered inauspicious. They can impact a person's life positively or negatively. The Navagraha gods and goddesses are observed in almost every Indian temple. They symbolize protection and are often engraved on the doors of temples. However, sometimes they are also marked on a separate pavilion or a raised platform in the temple as an image or idol.

Since the Vedic age, worshiping heavenly bodies was seen as a significant component of religious Hindu life. In every festival, marriage and yagna, offerings are proffered to the Navagraha. However, in certain contexts, some planets are not worshiped together due to their contrasting influences and characteristics. For example, Rahu and Ketu, which are shadow planets, are often considered opposites; their energies can create conflicting results in astrological interpretations. Similarly, the sun (Surya) and Saturn (Shani) may also be avoided in joint worship, as their energies can clash, potentially leading to challenges in one's life. Furthermore, these nine celestial bodies are also considered emitters or reflectors of rays of different colors, which have impact on a person's life. So, each of the Navagraha has a harmonious relationship with a specific color. Additionally, these heavenly bodies are also compatible with specific numbers and have a designated day of worship.

The Navagraha are:

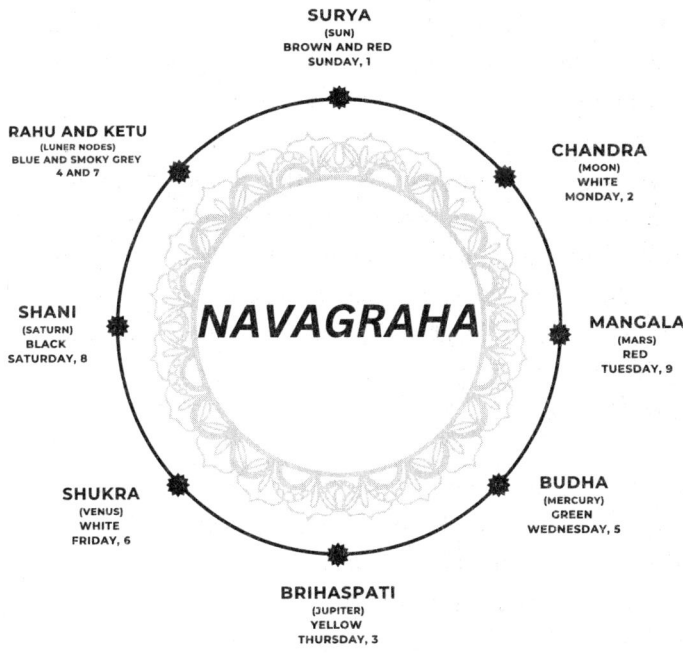

SURYA
(SUN)
BROWN AND RED
SUNDAY, 1

RAHU AND KETU
(LUNER NODES)
BLUE AND SMOKY GREY
4 AND 7

CHANDRA
(MOON)
WHITE
MONDAY, 2

SHANI
(SATURN)
BLACK
SATURDAY, 8

NAVAGRAHA

MANGALA
(MARS)
RED
TUESDAY, 9

SHUKRA
(VENUS)
WHITE
FRIDAY, 6

BUDHA
(MERCURY)
GREEN
WEDNESDAY, 5

BRIHASPATI
(JUPITER)
YELLOW
THURSDAY, 3

NAVAGRAHA ARE THE NINE CELESTIAL BODIES IN HINDU ASTROLOGY THAT ARE BELIEVED TO INFLUENCE HUMAN LIFE AND DESTINY.

Surya: He is the principal Vedic god. Generally, Navagraha is organized in the squire format, with Surya placed in the middle. It highlights the sun's impact on human life. Surya is the leader of all other planets in Hindu astrology. If Surya's position is indispensable in the person's astrological chart, it predicts power and success. It also emphasizes nobleness, courage, loyalty and pride. The number associated with Surya is one.

Chandra: The moon god, like Surya, is one of the main Vedic deities. He is the most important god in the Navagraha. According to astrology, any person born under Chandra's influence is religious, friendly, helpful, emotional and loyal. This god represents feminine nature with beauty and wisdom. The number associated with Chandra is two.

Mangala: Mars, or Mangala in the Navagraha, is a deity typically depicted with four hands and is regarded as a protector of dharma. Individuals born under the influence of Mangala are often characterized by qualities such as energy, confidence and, at times, assertiveness. Tuesday is traditionally the day set aside for the worship of Mangala, and the number associated with him is nine.

Budha: He is the son of the moon god. Green in color, he is depicted with four hands. Wednesday is the primary day of worship for Budha. This god also represents courage, strength, power and aggression. He is sometimes also designated as the god of war. It is assumed that a person born under the excellent planetary position of Budha, or Mercury, has Vishnu's blessings. The number associated with Budha is five.

Brihaspati: Jupiter is the guru of all the gods. In many Rigveda hymns, Brihaspati is praised. It is believed that any person born under Brihaspati's influence will have exceptional knowledge. This deity also symbolizes money, love and spirituality. Brihaspati is yellow or golden in color. The main day linked to him is Thursday and the number associated with him is three.

Shukra: The next Navagraha is the planet Venus, or Shukra. Shukra is a multifaceted figure who serves as one of the Saptarshis, as well as the guru of the asuras. As a revered sage, he embodies great wisdom and knowledge, while his role as the asura's teacher empowers him with secrets of Brahma Vidya. This god is represented in shades of golden. He holds a stick, a lotus and a set of bow and arrows in his hands. It is believed that any person born with Shukra as the ruling planet will have a luxurious life and good fortune. But for this person, charity is a must. Friday is the day for Shukra and the number associated with him is six.

Shani: Saturn or Shani is the son of Surya, and the day associated to him is Saturday. This planet is the most fatal to good fortune. If Shani has an unfavorable position in a person's astrological chart, they encounter many obstacles in their work. In accordance with some beliefs of Hinduism, many people do not travel or start their business on a Saturday. Depictions of Shani show him atop a buffalo, having four hands, holding a sword, an arrow and daggers. He is also at times considered a dark planet that negatively impacts peoples' lives, making them miserable. There are many temples dedicated to him across India. A person's life is rewarded or punished appropriately during their life as per their deeds, and Shani is in charge of the supervision. The number associated with Shani is eight.

Rahu and Ketu: They are regarded as both devas and asuras. These shadow planets are found in the north and south nodes of an eclipse. Rahu and Ketu overshadow the sun and the moon through eclipses. The former is depicted as a black figure siting on a golden chariot, which is pulled by eight horses. The latter with his snake-like body rides on a vulture. As per Hindu legends, during the Samudra Manthan, the asura Rahu disguised himself as a god and drank the divine nectar. Learning about this, Vishnu's female avatar, Mohini, cut off his head. But Rahu had already tasted the nectar, despite having had his head chopped off, he became immortal. As he had been seated between Surya and Chandra, this incident had an unfortunate influence on the sun and the moon in the form of the eclipses. There is no day dedicated to Rahu or Ketu. Their influence on a person's horoscope can lead to suffering or obstacles in progress. In Hindu scriptures, the eclipses are assumed to be an evil omen. Ketu is the representation of karmic collections for both good and bad, spiritual and supernatural influences. The numbers associated with Rahu and Ketu are mostly four and seven, respectively.

The group of nine heavenly bodies constitute a set of deities, and some demons. They are said to influence a person's life, career, wealth and health. The three bodies, Shani, Rahu and Ketu, are seldom considered sinister but can also have an unfavorable impact on a person's life.

TUTELARY AND
FOLK GODS

Throughout India's length and breadth, many great gods from the Hindu pantheon have been forgotten or are slowly fading from people's memories. One such example is Brahma, the creator. Presently, there are very few temples that are dedicated to him. Another example is Indra, one of the most venerated gods of the Vedic age and early Hinduism, who now has been reduced to being portrayed as an egotistical god; in some villages, he is solely honored as a weather godling. There is also Agni, the intermediary between humans and the divine, and a crucial deity during yagnas, whose importance is waning due to the decline of traditional Vedic rituals in modern times. Instead, many unique gods and demigods have emerged in India in the last thousand years or so.

This can be another classification of gods in Hinduism—some of these deities are worshiped mainly by local, regional or other distinct communities. Tutelary deities are supernatural beings who are as holy, sacred and divine as the supreme gods but are honored by a few people, or for a specific purpose. They exist at the folk, regional and, sometimes, at the national level, all over the country. Some evil demigods are also a part of this list. Tutelary gods are mostly worshiped in India's tiny hamlets, but their worship is an essential component of Hinduism. These gods are of different types, like Ishta Devata, Kul Devi or Kul Devata, ancient sages and folk gods. Folk Hinduism consists of worshiping the local and regional deities, as they fulfill the community's basic and immediate needs. Generally, these gods have a distinct purpose. They are revered for specific causes; for instance, the goddess of cholera helps in treating that particular disease. Although there is no definite demarcation, most tutelary gods have unique characteristics and qualities:

Regional: Tutelary gods are worshiped in a specific place, temple or area. One cannot find many temples or shrines of these gods across India. Also, they do not have multiple incarnations.

For Specific Needs: These gods are worshiped for a particular requirement, like good weather, cures for diseases, black magic or some other very specific reason. Everyone reveres them despite their differences in caste or creed in the region.

Super Humans: Tutelary gods and goddesses have superhuman qualities. They are merciful and protective of their devotees. But sometimes they can be ill-tempered, angry and impatient. They are mostly represented as human beings, or half-humans wherein their other half can be an object or an aspect of nature.

Apart from the general characteristics, rituals specific to these tutelary gods are their sole differentiating factor. It will not be possible to include all the Hindu tutelary gods in this book, as there are thousands of them across India. Sometimes, the same tutelary god is worshiped in a different place, with a new name, but with similar narratives and customs. It should be noted that both male and female tutelary gods are given equal importance. The tutelary goddesses are nurturing, healing and protective. They symbolize purity but can also punish. In Puranic scriptures, many tutelary goddesses are called Devi or Mata, and they have a great number of followers. I have included below some tutelary gods who are widely worshiped, and some who might not be as well known.

SHITALA
The Goddess of Smallpox

Considered an avatar of Parvati, Shitala is widely worshiped, especially in northern and central India and some parts of Nepal and Pakistan. Shitala means "calm or cool" in Sanskrit. She helps break the fevers of patients and relieves them of their ailments. Shitala has the power to cure diseases and people to this day continue to have a lot of faith in her. She is believed to cure poxes, skin diseases, sores, fever and other infectious diseases, and is most directly linked with smallpox. Even though science and religion are like oil and water, sometimes they can be in close proximity to each other in harmonious ways.

Shitala is worshiped on Shitala Ashtami, the eighth day after Holi, to rid the world of all illnesses. On this day, it is recommended that fire not be lit in the kitchen. So, food is usually prepared the previous day. It is also consumed by the household only after offering it to the goddess first. This food, which is cooked a day before, is called basoda. Furthermore, during festivities for Shitala, heating the food is avoided and sexual activities are minimized. This festival is majorly celebrated in states like Rajasthan, Bengal, Uttar Pradesh and Madhya Pradesh. The temples of Shitala are mostly in Bengal, and in many states of north and central India. Her other names are Shitala Mata and Sitalamangal, and in some parts of south India, Shitala is known as Mariamma.

Interestingly, Mata is another common word for smallpox. It means "mother" and, as mentioned earlier, is used as a respectful affix for the goddess. Sometimes, she is worshiped in the form of a demigoddess. She is portrayed with two to four hands, and usually holds a conch, a pot and some neem leaves. This goddess does not have a spouse. Shitala is revered by everyone, but she specifically attends to and provides assistance to the poor. According to a famous tale from medieval folklore, she had around six sisters: Masani, Mahaimati, Polamde, Lamkaria, Basanti and Agwani, who were primarily associated with other types of fevers in different regions of India.

If a person is suffering from poxes in villages where Shitala is worshiped, then neem is used as a cure. Similarly, branches of the neem tree are hung in the doorway for curing children infected by smallpox. It is believed that Shitala uses the neem leaves and sprinkles the holy water from her kalash or pot on the patient to heal them. In many parts of rural India, this practice is followed, the benefit of which is scientifically proven. The neem tree, *Azadirachta Indica*, is an effective remedy for the disease. These leaves are organic and have medicinal properties, owing to their timber. Hence, the sufferer's body is rubbed or coated with neem, and they are given cooling beverages.

Shitala is prominently mentioned in various scriptures, especially in the Skanda Purana, where she is known as the goddess of smallpox. According to legend, Shitala not only created the disease but also holds the unique power to cure it. It is said that Brahma, the creator, instructed her to help humans by curing illnesses caused by germs, filth and high temperatures. In her early days, Shitala cared for the devas, nursing them back to health when they were afflicted by the disease. Eventually, she descended to Earth to assist humanity directly.

One famous tale narrates the story of a time when a small kingdom ruled by King Birat was struck by a devastating outbreak of smallpox. Everyone in the kingdom fell ill. In their time of need, Shitala appeared before the king and urged him to worship her. As the people began to honor the goddess through prayers and rituals, Shitala gradually lifted the disease from the land, restoring health and happiness to the kingdom. Through devotion, the people learned the power of faith and the importance of honoring the divine, making Shitala a beloved figure in their lives.

MANASA DEVI
The Snake Goddess

Snakes connote mystery and danger. Unsurprisingly, they are usually not accepted within human territories. However, the serpents in Hindu lore have a strong religious significance. Since the early Vedic and Puranic periods, snakes have been worshiped in various forms. Many mythological texts provide insights into snake worship. Snake worship is even mentioned in the Ramayana and Mahabharata. In Hinduism, snakes are worshiped in temples and are offered milk, oil and incense sticks. The hood of a snake is denoted by the word "phana," which refers to the venom used by the creature to kill its prey. Nagas, beings that are half-human and half-serpent, have always held a notable place in Hindu legends and folklore.

The tutelary goddess Manasa Devi is the goddess of snakes. Sometimes she is referred to as Vishahari or fertility goddess, meaning "the destroyer of poison." She can prevent and cure snakebites and also boost fertility. Manasa Devi is mentioned in various scriptures that present a paradoxical narrative. In some texts, she is the daughter of Shiva and Paravati. But in other instances, she is noted as the daughter of Kashyapa. Manasa Devi is also regarded as the sister of Vasuki Naga, who was used by the devas and asuras to churn the cosmic ocean. The goddess is also mentioned in the Shiva Purana and the Mahabharata. Consequently, the story of her origin varies.

Manasa Devi, though known for her compassion toward her followers, is believed to have a fiery temper toward those who commit wrongdoings. She is mostly depicted as a woman wrapped with snakes, sitting on a lotus or standing on top of snakes. Her figure is at times shown as sheltered under the hoods of seven cobras. Interestingly, in certain parts of India, she is even worshiped sans any kind of imagery. She is prominently worshiped in Bengal, Assam, Andhra Pradesh and Tripura. Her temple in Haridwar is a Shakti Peetha and is famous for fulfilling wishes of the devotees. The festival, Naga Panchami is celebrated to worship Manasa Devi. On this day, people fast and offer milk to snakes in many villages of India.

Other snake gods in Hinduism are Nageshwara, Vasuki Naga, Shesha Naga and Takshaka Naga. They each have their own significance and particularities, and their disciples can be found in different parts of India. Snake worship has been common across various regions of India and is prevalent in almost all the tribes of the country. The figure of nagas originally arose from snakes in ancient Hindu scriptures. Numerous famous mythological stories are associated with these guardians of hidden treasures, which are usually priceless gems called Nagamani.

HINGLAJ MATA
Devi in Balochistan

A form of Sati and Durga, Hinglaj Mata is another important tutelary goddess. She is a Kul Devi for many Hindu families in India and Pakistan. Her temple is a prominent Hindu pilgrimage site near the Hingol River in the rough hills of Balochistan, Pakistan.

Hinglaj is one of the most remote Hindu pilgrimage destinations in the world. Many pilgrims opine that the road to Hinglaj is one of the toughest to traverse in history. Devotees embark on a journey of over six weeks, traveling from Karachi on camels through the hot, arid desert of Pakistan, facing numerous obstacles along the way. The popular belief is that the pilgrim will either receive death or darshan on their way to the site. Once pilgrims arrive in Hinglaj they complete a series of rituals, like climbing the Chandragup and Khandewari mud volcanoes. Devotees throw coconuts into the craters in the Chandragup mud volcano to make wishes and thank the gods for answering their prayers. Shiva is also worshiped in this Shakti Peetha as Bhairava.

The origin of Hinglaj is related to Sati. Sati is believed to have been very beautiful, but it was with her penance and devotion that won Shiva's heart. She left the comforts of her father's palace to live a simple and austere life in the forest, dedicated as she was to her spiritual journey with Shiva. As per a popular legend, King Daksha, the father of Sati, was not happy with Shiva; he was upset that his daughter married an ascetic, someone who lived in the mountains in the company of ghosts and animals, against his will. Hence, King Daksha broke all ties with Sati. One time, he decided to perform an exceptional yagna, and invited all the gods, family and friends, but not Shiva and Sati. Sati was furious but Daksha refused to change his mind. Sati flew into such a rage that she jumped into the yagna in protest and burned herself to death. Distraught by the sacrifice of his dearest wife, Shiva began to dance the devastating Tandava. The whole world started shaking. All the deities, including King Daksha, begged him to show mercy and stop. Finally, the god obliged.

It is believed he performed the Tandava with Sati's ashes, which caused her ashes to scatter; they fell at different points on Earth. All the places where the ashes dropped turned holy and are now known as Shakti Peethas. Some of these places have become major pilgrimage sites, as the goddess-oriented Shakti sect embraces them. Supposedly, Sati's ashes fell in 51 different places on Earth. Hinglaj is one of those places, and is considered an important Shakti Peetha, particularly for those seeking healing and protection.

Karni Mata is considered the incarnation of Hinglaj and sometimes also of Durga. She is the Kul Devi of many Rajasthani families and of many people in the neighboring areas of Haryana and Gujarat. A famous temple dedicated to her is quite peculiar, as it is the only temple where not only are the premises overrun with thousand of rats but the rodents are actually worshiped by the devotees. This temple is called Karni Mata Temple, and it is located in Bikaner, Rajasthan. The rats in this temple are considered children, and the pilgrims feed them milk, coconut and grains. Emerging during the medieval period, Karni Mata was known as Riddhi Bai. There are many other temples dedicated to her across Rajasthan. In fact, visited by thousands, a famous Karni Mata fair is held twice a year at these temples.

KHATU SHYAM
The Truly Divine

Khatu Shyam, popularly known as Shyam Baba or Barbareeka, is an important tutelary god, immensely worshiped in modern times owing to his supernatural powers. Barbareeka was a yaksha, reborn as a man to Ghatotkacha and Ahilawati, making him the grandson of Hidimbi and Bhima, the second eldest and most powerful of the Pandavas. It is said that he witnessed the Kurukshetra war in the Mahabharata without taking part in it.

He was a brave warrior and learned the art of war from his grandmother. As a blessing, Shiva gave him three arrows. He was so powerful that he could have won the battle at Kurukshetra singlehandedly in less than a day, with just those three arrows. But because of his strong sense of virtue he always chose to support the disadvantaged side in conflicts, reflecting his commitment to helping those in need and upholding justice. That is why another well-known title for him is Haare ka Sahara, which translates to "supporter of the losing side." Agni had also bestowed him with a boon, ensuring he would always be victorious across the three worlds and remain undefeatable. Khatu Shyam was also a deeply benevolent man, who never denied anyone's request.

In the Mahabharata tale, Krishna knew that if Barbareeka participated in the war, he would side with the Kauravas, thereby defeating the Pandavas. So as a favor, Krishna asked Barbareeka for his head. Barbareeka acceded to Krishna's request and the god was immensely moved by this sacrifice. So, in return Krishna granted him a boon, which caused Barbareeka to be worshiped in the Kali Yuga as Khatu Shyam. Hence, he is famously known as Sheesh Ke Daani, meaning "the one who donated his head to Krishna."

In this iteration of the tale, even after decapitating himself, Barbareeka wished to see the war. Hence, Krishna placed his head on the summit of a hill, from where he could view the entire battlefield. It is believed that Barbareeka offered up his head to Krishna in Sikar, Rajasthan, which is why this place has a famous temple named Khatu Shyam Temple dedicated to him. Every year millions of pilgrims visit the temple. Shukla Ekadashi and Dwadashi, the eleventh and twelfth day of the the waxing phase of the moon of every month, as per the Hindu calendar, are the days for the worship of Khatu Shyam. People believe that on Shukla Dwadashi, Barbareeka donated his head to Krishna. During these auspicious days, thousands of devotees visit the temple.

In another tale, after the war was over, the Pandavas were engaged in fierce debate over who among them was the most skilled warrior. Krishna suggested they ask Barbareeka's head, as he had witnessed the entire war. Thus, Bhima went to the top of the hill and asked Barbareeka. He replied that all he could see and recognize was Krishna; his divine Sudarshana

Chakra rotated on the battlefield and killed the unrighteous and wicked people. As per him, the Pandavas were merely pretending and not actually fighting the war.

Barbareeka is worshiped in many parts of India, especially in Rajasthan as Khatu Shyam. However, Barbareeka's story is not found in Veda Vyas' Mahabharata—it actually comes from the Skanda Purana. He is not an incarnation of Vishnu. Instead, he is assumed to be a great devotee of Krishna. It is quite fascinating to see stickers of the three arrows on vehicles or banners, symbolizing Khatu Shyam, near Jaipur and surrounding towns. The deity is also renowned in Nepal, where he is known as King Yalambar.

RANI SATI
The Devoted Wife, Warrior and Demigoddess

Rani Sati, usually known as Dadiji, is another tutelary goddess. She is believed to be an incarnation of Sati, who symbolizes self-immolation. People started worshiping her during the medieval period. But a narrative related to this figure is known and has been in circulation since the time of the Mahabharata. Uttara, Abhimanyu's wife, desired to follow the custom of sati, which involved burning oneself on the funeral pyre of one's husband. But Uttara could not do so because she was pregnant. She asked Krishna if, in her next life, she could get married to Abhimanyu again and perform the sati ritual. After many prayers and entreaties, Krishna finally granted her the boon. After 13 centuries, Uttara was reborn as Narayani, and she performed sati after her husband's death, who had been reborn as Tandhan. In a battle with a king, Tandhan had killed the king's son. Later, the king sought revenge by killing him in front of his wife, Narayani. As an act of vengeance, she defeated her husband's killer in battle. After winning the fight, she decided to set herself ablaze on Tandhan's funeral pyre. Narayani was considered an exceptional woman, a great warrior who was highly respected. She later became a demigoddess.

Devotees continue to pay tribute to her. She is popularly known as Rani Sati, and there is a famous temple in Rajasthan built in her honor—the Rani Sati Dadi temple. Due to disputes over certain practices, the temple was possibly shut down for some point of time, but the devotees, to this day, continue to trust the place and its miracles. They believe Rani Sati, the guardian mother of every woman in the nearby villages protects her worshipers and fulfills their desires.

Rani Sati temples can be found in different cities of India. The oldest temple is in Kolkata, and the biggest one is in the Jhunjhunu district of Rajasthan. Many institutions have tried to shut down this temple and stop Sati Puja because sati is a crime under the Commission for Sati [Prevention] Act of 1987. But millions of devotees continue to visit this temple every year. It is important to note that the practice of sati was not mentioned in any Vedic scriptures. It started only during the medieval period.

NARADA MUNI
The First Journalist on Earth

Narada Muni, the Vedic seer, is a famous musician, storyteller and messenger of the gods in many mythological stories of the Puranas and epics. Narada Muni is popularly known as the one who dispenses news and wisdom to everyone. He is a demigod who possesses all the knowledge of this world. Commonly referred to as Rishiraj, the king of all rishis, he is mostly depicted carrying a vina and a kartal, while wearing a saffron piece of cloth. He has a boon that allows him to travel across the three worlds at his will without any obstacles, and he does not need a vahana or a structure of any kind to do so. Narada Muni is acknowledged as the child of Brahma and Saraswati. He is often misunderstood and unjustly accused of inciting hatred, which can lead to conflicts among the devas and, sometimes, asuras. However, these claims misrepresent his true nature. As a gifted storyteller endowed with the knowledge of the past, present and future, he uses his wisdom to convey important lessons and inspire devotion. His intent is not to provoke strife, but to enlighten and guide others through his narratives.

Interestingly, it was supposedly Narada Muni who had asked Valmiki to write the Ramayana. He narrated the complete story, with all the relevant details and events, which enabled Valmiki to write it down. It had happened on a day Narada Muni had gone to the hermitage of Valmiki. During a discussion on the Vedas, Valmiki asked Narada Muni if there was anyone on Earth who had unerringly continued on the path of righteousness their entire life, even amid difficulties; he enquired if there was anyone who was considered an ideal person, king, child, husband or brother? The sage asked if anyone was that noble, pious, honest, tenacious and had devoted their entire life to dharma.

Narada Muni replied that the person was Rama, the king of Ayodhya, who was an avatar of Vishnu and had incarnated to set an example for humankind. Thereafter, he narrated the entire story of Rama (known as the Sankshepa Ramayana), and Valmiki was convinced that he was indeed the most incredible being on Earth, through all of time. With the story, Valmiki started writing the Ramayana, and soon it became one of the world's greatest epics.

There is much lore about Narada Muni. In some stories, it is mentioned that he once cursed Vishnu so that he may be forced to stay away from women. Consequently, Vishnu was incarnated in the form of Rama, and as the Ramayana tells us, he had to undergo a long period of separation from Sita.

Narada Muni is also known for singing devotional songs that glorify the divine and for dedicating his life to worship. The Narada Purana, while considered a minor Purana, holds significant spiritual value. Although there are relatively few temples dedicated to Narada Muni in India, he continues to be revered and worshiped to this day. His influence endures through the devotion and teachings he inspires in his followers.

LESSER-KNOWN TUTELARY GODS

Thousands of tutelary and folk gods in Hinduism are unrelated to any specific deity or god. Many are honored by a few people, in some particular rural communities only. It is not within the scope of this book to provide a comprehensive list of all such tutelary gods but some of the unique ones are mentioned below.

Iravan, son of Arjuna: Iravan, a secondary character from the Mahabharata, was the son of Arjuna and the Naga princess, Ulupi. He is one of the main gods for the Kuttantavar. Iravan is majorly worshiped in some parts of Tamil Nadu. He is famous amongst the transgender communities in India. Iravan sacrificed himself to Kali to cement the victory of the Pandavas. Though not as famous as his half-brother Abhimanyu, he was also a great warrior. Iravan wanted to marry before his death and Krishna fulfilled this wish by transforming into his female form, Mohini. Even today in some remote parts of India, an 18–day festival is celebrated under different names, like Koovagam, to pay tribute to Iravan whose severed head is worshiped. He is also revered in countries like Indonesia, Nepal and Bali. Iravan is associated with many mythological stories, and some are similar to those about Khatu Shyam.

Khodiyar Maa: This warrior goddess is majorly worshiped in Gujarat and Rajasthan by some specific communities. The worship of Khodiyar Maa is estimated to have started around 700 CE. One among seven daughters, she was born after Shiva blessed her parents. A brave woman, her birth name was Janbai. She is depicted as a young woman dressed in Indian attire with a Trishul in her hands. Her vahana is a crocodile. She is often offered porridge as prasada.

The story of Khodiyar is an especially popular tale in Gujarati folklore that highlights bravery, devotion and sacrifice. However, she is a beloved goddess in various other communities as well.

In the Gujarati folk story, while playing by a pond, Janbai's brother is bitten by a venomous snake. To save him, she bravely attempts to seeks out the snake and get some of the venom from it. A divine crocodile, known as a magar, comes forth to assist her. With its help, Janbai descends into the Patal Lok (the underworld) to confront the snake and save her brother.

During her journey, she injures her foot on a large rock, which is where her name Khodiyar, meaning "one whose feet are injured," originates. Despite the pain, her courage leads her to successfully save her brother, and this act of bravery solidifies her status as a protector and a goddess in the eyes of her devotees. The story emphasizes themes of familial love, courage in the face of danger and divine assistance.

This is why the crocodile is regarded as the vahana of Khodiyar Maa. The goddess is known by various names in different parts of Gujarat and Rajasthan. Similar such stories narrate her triumph over evil and her bravery, which saved the lives of other people in her region. There are many temples dedicated to Khodiyar Maa, and every year thousands of devotees visit them to protect themselves from evil. It is believed that whenever any devotee of Khodiyar Maa is in trouble, she always keeps them from harm.

Kamadeva: The Hindu god of love is portrayed mostly with his female counterpart, Rati. Brahma created Kamadeva from his mind to spread love in the world by shooting flower arrows. Often depicted as a youthful figure with a bow made of sugarcane and arrows adorned with flowers, the god of love is associated with the emotional and romantic aspects of life. He plays a significant role in various legends, including the famous tale where Brahma got angry when Kama used his first arrow against the creator himself. Hence, he cursed Kama that in the future he would be burnt to ashes by Shiva. However, after much pleading by Kama, Brahma assured him of rebirth; he would be reincarnated at the mercy of Shiva, under a different name—Madana. Later, because of the curse, he attempted to disrupt the meditation of Shiva to bring him back to the world of love, following the god's intense penance because of the death of Sati.

Kamadeva embodies the beauty and intricacies of love and attraction. People worship him to honor love and romantic relationships, as he serves as a reminder of both the joys and challenges that come with this emotion.

Shashthi Devi: This folk goddess takes care of newborn babies and the health of children, for she is considered to be the protector of young ones. She is also the deity of vegetation and reproduction, and is widely regarded as the benefactor of households. The goddess has many names, like Shashthimata,

Devi Shashthi and Shashthika. References to this goddess appear in Hindu scriptures as early as the eighth and ninth century BCE, in which she is associated with children and the Hindu war god Skanda. Shashthi Devi is also related to various other goddesses in Hinduism. Women used to walk in forests, collect and eat fruit, and offer prayers to Shashthi Devi for healthy and beautiful children.

Shashthi Devi is portrayed as a young, motherly woman with one, two or, sometimes, eight infants in her arms. She is mainly worshiped on Ashoka Shashthi, which is celebrated on the sixth day of Chaitra Shukla Paksha in northern India. On this day, women drink water from six flower buds of the ashoka tree to secure their children's well-being. In Bengal and south India, it is known as Aranya Shashthi that falls again on the sixth day of Jyeshtha Shukla Paksha. Additionally, Khas Shashthi is celebrated on the sixth day of Paush Shukla Paksha. A fast is observed and the goddess is worshiped for the long life of children.

Oladevi: She is the goddess of cholera and is an important goddess of the folk tradition in Bengal. Oladevi is considered the wife of Mangal in some interpretations, while in others, she is portrayed as a protective goddess who battles against him. This duality reflects the complex nature of her character in folklore: it emphasizes her role in combating disease while also being linked to Mangal, as the battle against him to protect the people highlights the struggle between good and evil. During cholera outbreaks in the past centuries, she was revered to protect people from the disease in rural areas. Oladevi is frequently depicted as Lakshmi with yellow skin, sometimes wearing a blue sari and lots of gold ornaments. She used to be worshiped on Saturday by people in the region of Bengal and Bangladesh, but the significance of her worship has diminished in recent times. This is likely due to a decrease in cholera outbreaks because of progress in medicine and improvements in general sanitation.

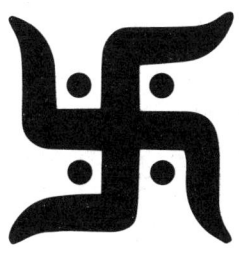

SIGNS, SYMBOLS
AND SOUNDS IN
HINDUISM

Symbols have held profound significance throughout ancient history for various reasons. They often serve as tangible representations of beliefs and concepts, allowing individuals to connect with the divine and their faith. These sacred symbols reinforce cultural and communal identities, surpassing linguistic barriers to unite people under shared religious concepts.

The Christian cross, also known as the Crux Immissa, stands as one of the most important religious symbols in history, representing the crucifixion of Jesus Christ and the core beliefs of Christianity, including sacrifice, redemption and hope. Its origins can be traced back to prehistoric times, to the use of two plain, unadorned sticks that were crossed to form a simple shape. Initially adopted by a small group, the symbol eventually gained global prominence within Christianity, signifying love, sacrifice and redemption. Similarly, the Greek cross, characterized by arms of equal length intersecting at right angles, adorned numerous Greek artifacts, exemplifying balance and divine order.

In Norse mythology, Mjolnir, Thor's hammer, was depicted as an upside-down cross, representing both its powerful force and Thor's protective role in Norse culture. Remarkably, Mjolnir is recognized today by the US Department of Veteran Affairs as a symbol of cultural significance—it can be engraved on the graves of soldiers who have died in active duty.

Across the globe, these symbols have transcended geographical and cultural boundaries, embodying concepts from life and immortality to spiritual protection and cosmic order. They continue to play pivotal roles in connecting individuals with their faith, fostering collective identities and preserving cultural traditions through the ages.

Adding on to these examples is one of the oldest and most popular symbols in human history, the swastika. Found across different continents and cultures, much before other symbols came into being, the swastika embodies diverse meanings, including life, prosperity and spiritual well-being. Its enduring presence underscores its universal significance across ancient civilizations.

THE AUSPICIOUS
SYMBOL OF THE SWASTIKA

The swastika has been discovered in archaeological findings dating back thousands of years, across multiple locations and civilizations. It has been found in artifacts from the ancient Indus Valley civilization, particularly at sites like Harappa and Mohenjo-daro. Similarly, the symbol has also been discovered in Europe, dating back to the Neolithic period in Ukraine, Greece and other European countries. Similar symbols have been found in Central Asia among the remains of the Scythians and Samaritans as well.

Many investigations have been conducted to find out the possible reasons behind the symbol's appearance across the world. However, much of the evidence of its origins points to India. This sacred symbol holds great importance in Hinduism and is still worshiped by millions. According to the research done by scholars from IIT-Kharagpur on ancient Indian knowledge systems: "The ancient Indian Swastika is therefore 11000 years old or even [*sic*] earlier, predating any Aryan invasion, and evident in many ancient Palaeolithic Indian rock art forms."[17]

The swastika has various names across different countries and cultures, such as manji in ancient China and Japan, the fylfot cross in Christianity and tetraskelion in ancient Greece. However, it is important to note that these symbols are not identical to the Hindu swastika; rather, they are variations, reverse or even flipped versions, of the same design. Each interpretation carries its own cultural significance and meaning, reflecting the diverse ways in which this ancient symbol has been utilized throughout history. Subsequently, every country and civilization accepted the Sanskrit name swastika, which became its universal name. In Sanskrit, swastika means "all is well." It is the combination of "su," which means "good," and "asti," meaning to "exist." It is a symbol of auspiciousness and good fortune.

In Hinduism, this symbol was revered long before any other symbols of Shiva or Vishnu. Like the swastika's origin, several theories about its connection to the ancient Hindu deities have also been presented. It is sometimes estimated that the symbol is related to Surya, Agni and, occasionally, even Indra, the Vedic period's primary god. The swastika is also associated with all four Vedas and the Hindu life principles of kama, artha and moksha. Sometimes, the four sides of the symbol, pointing in the four directions, are interpreted as the four Yugas: Satya Yuga, Treta Yuga, Dvapara Yuga and Kali Yuga.

The swastika is represented as a straightforward cross with straight lines of uniform thickness. These lines intersect at right angles, dividing the design into four equal segments. Notably, each end extends outward at 90-degree angles, ensuring symmetry and a consistent direction throughout the shape. Besides that, they are drawn with dots at intersections and sometimes, the lines are curved at the tip. The swastika moves in a clockwise direction, whereas the left-handed, or anticlockwise shape, is the aswastika, which is believed to bring negative energy.

It is said that hanging a swastika on the main door of a house brings prosperity. Hence, one can find the symbol in almost every Hindu house and temple in the present day. At times, if a person belonging to the Hindu faith purchases a new vehicle, the swastika symbol is drawn on the vehicle. As per Vastu Shastra, the symbol is crucial for attracting positive energy to one's homestead. If there are any defects in the house or negative energy, the swastika reduces those effects. Color is another crucial factor for these geometric figures: white, red, orange and blue are the shades most commonly used. A swastika is usually drawn using red vermilion or turmeric.

THE SACRED SOUND OF AUM

Aum, also written as om, is one of the most sacred and oft-chanted syllables in Hinduism. For thousands of years, most Hindus have begun their day by chanting "aum." The symbol can be found at the top of all Hindu religious writings, on wedding invitation cards, business journals, trading reports, publications and wall paintings. People even tattoo it on their body. In fact, across India, people can be seen wearing aum pendants. In almost all Hindu temples, festivals, rituals, offerings, worships, yagnas and sanskaras, one comes across this sacred symbol, which is also added as a prefix to, and is a part of, almost all the Hindu mantras. In Sanskrit, the three primary syllables—A-U-M—are combined to create the sound of "aum," which is a mantra in itself. Hence, aum is considered the root mantra. Additionally, aum, the syllable, is also referred to as omkara. Thus, it will not be incorrect to say that it is the most essential and sacred symbol of Hinduism and all its sects.

Aum was first introduced in the Vedas. Later, it was found in almost all other Hindu scriptures, especially in the Upanishads like Mandukya, Chandogya, Taittiriya and Atharvashikha. Many other minor Upanishads, Puranas, and the Mahabharat and the Ramayana deliberate upon the symbol's importance. For example, the very first mantra of the Mandukya Upanishad states:

ओमित्येतदक्षरमिदं सर्व तस्योपव्याख्यानं ।
भूतं भवद् भविष्यदिति सर्वमोङ्कार एव ।
यच्चान्यत् त्रिकालातीतं तदप्योङ्कार एव ॥

Omityetadaksaramidam sarvam tasyopavyakhyanam,
Bhutam bhavad bhavisyat iti sarvam onkara eva,
Yaccanyat trikalatitam tadapyonkara eva.

Translation

Aum is the everlasting word that has everything, aum is the universe, the past, the present and the future. All that was, all that is, all that will be beyond time is the word aum.

—*Mandukya Upanishad, Verse 1*

The complete Mandukya Upanishad has only 12 mantras and it primarily revolves around aum, as a mantra, while focusing on the self. Most of the Vedic mantras start with aum as a prefix.

Following are the different manifestations of this symbol:

Aum and Ganesha: Aum written in Sanskrit often casts the image of Ganesha. If we closely notice the upper curve, it looks like the side view of his head, especially with the twisted angle as his trunk. Similarly, the bottom curve represents the belly of the god.

Aum and the Brahman: It has long been believed that aum's vibration and sound are behind the creation of the whole universe and the soul. While practicing the pranava meditation, the primary aim is to focus one's mind on the aum sound.

Aum and the Trideva: Aum is also the symbol of the Trinity. It represents the three aspects of Brahma, Vishnu and Shiva. "A" stands for Creation—Brahma, "U" endures for Preservation—Vishnu and "M" experiences Dissolution—Shiva.

Alternatively, aum also represents the three tattvas: rajas or activity, tamas or destruction and sattva or purity. It often explores concepts found in the Upanishads, which discuss the relationship between the individual soul, atman, and Brahman, the universal spirit. It is sometimes called a beej mantra[18] or seed mantra. By chanting it, one connects with an inner awareness where the syllable "A" represents the waking state, "U" refers to the dream state and "M" is the unconscious state or a form of hibernation of one's mind.

Various scientific studies, along with evidence from both traditional practices and modern research, collectively provide insights into the benefits of chanting aum and its potential effects on mental, emotional and spiritual well-being. Furthermore, chanting the word also reduces depression and provides strength. One can feel purity, concentration, power of life and consciousness while doing so. The rhythmic pronunciations awaken spirituality and ensure self-realization. Chanting enhances memory and increases attentiveness in all age groups. It facilitates spiritual enlightenment and reduces stress related to hypertension. Research carried out on the mantra by the Indian Council of Medical Research (ICMR) Centre for Advanced Research in Yoga and Neurophysiology showed that the people who chanted the aum mantra during meditation displayed improved mental attentiveness and physiological relaxation. The research states: "The neurohemodynamic correlates of 'OM' chanting indicate limbic deactivation. As similar observations have been recorded with vagus nerve stimulation treatment used in depression and epilepsy, the study findings argue for a potential role of this 'OM' chanting in clinical practice."[19]

During meditation, chanting aum generates specific vibrations that resonate within the body and mind, creating a sense of harmony and connection to the cosmos. This sound is believed to align with the universal energy, facilitating a deeper meditative experience. The rhythmic repetition of aum helps quiet worldly thoughts and distractions, allowing practitioners to focus inward and cultivate mindfulness. As the sound reverberates, it promotes relaxation by easing muscle tension and calming the nervous system, contributing to an overall sense of peace and well-being. This practice not only enhances mental clarity and emotional stability but also fosters a profound spiritual connection, making it a powerful tool for practicing deeper states of meditation.

YANTRA, THE MYSTICAL DIAGRAM

Due to the numerous scriptures and their vibrant discourse, Hinduism has adopted more spiritual symbols, diagrams and icons than any other religion. Their significance goes beyond mere weapons, vahanas, offerings or ornaments. The rich array of iconography in Hinduism helps deepen the connection between human consciousness and profound wisdom. The symbols are used to comprehend things beyond the mind's restrictive and limited understanding. Similarly, the unconscious mind as an inner language creates a natural affinity with the metaphysical world. Every god of Hinduism has one or more icons and symbols associated with it. The Vedic gods, the Trimurti and the tutelary gods have their respective signs, logos and icons. These icons and symbols are worshiped in Hinduism as a representation of that particular god.

The symbols and icons used for religious representation, such as the swastika, om (aum), and yajnashala (sacrificial altar), were foundational to early prayer practices that originated in the Vedic period and gained prominence during the Puranic period.

In the Puranic period, new symbols and figures, such as the bindu, triangle and fish became widely recognized. Additionally, various animals, plants, weapons and colors associated with the gods gained sacred significance. For example, the lotus flower emerged as a symbol of the universe's origin, while the shankha became important in prayers, particularly in worshiping Vishnu and his incarnations. Overall, this also demonstrates how the use of symbols evolved from the initial prayer practices of the Vedic period to the more prominent and diverse representations found in the Puranic period, highlighting the deepening relationship between symbolism and spirituality in Hinduism.

Just like sacred symbols, the holy diagrams also transformed into representations of gods and were used along with mantras for prayers in Hinduism. These diagrams are called yantras. These sacred geometrical diagrams represent specific gods and mantras. Yantras became a part of worship in the later Puranic period. These sacred diagrams are worshiped, by chanting mantras, as a manifestation of God. Hence, a yantra is like a body, and its soul is the mantra that should be chanted for the purpose of worshiping the diagram. Yantras are worshiped at homes, shops, temples, and anywhere and everywhere in Hinduism. They are also used for meditation and the safeguarding of health and wealth.

In fact, the power of these yantras is infinite. Understanding and tapping into the potential of the yantras is not easy for every Hindu. The secret lies in the proper recitation of hymns, prayers or mantras along with performing other rituals. Some symbols and geometric figures are considered directly related to the universe's evolution. They can potentially channel a power source when created correctly. A yantra can be two- or three-dimensional and is created from a center point which is called a bindu or a dot. Therefore, these diagrams are associated with the universe, or the creation of all things.

Yantras are mainly worshiped in the Tantric tradition of Hinduism. Tantrism was a diversionary movement as it contradicted the Vedic religious practices. Its origin can be traced back to the fifth or sixth century CE. The primary purpose of this movement is to escape the endless cycle of life, death and rebirth in order to attain moksha or mukti. Yoga and meditation were the main principles of Tantric worship and rituals. The main Tantric goddess is Shakti or Kali i.e., the energy that created everything in this universe. There are many forms of gods and goddesses in Tantrism. The following is mentioned in the book *Shakti and Shakta*: "There is a feeling that the Tantra Shastra is related only to Shakti or devi worship which is partially correct. There are Tantras of other sects of the Agama, Tantras of Shaivas, and Vaishnavas."[20]

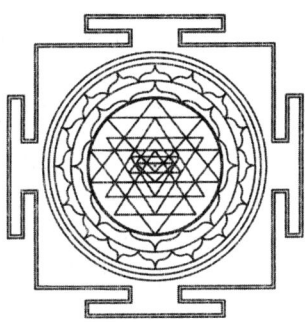

There are many types of yantras with distinct geometric designs. They are associated with multiple gods, principles and planets. Parallelly, geometric configurations of symbols are also seen in other religions like Buddhism, Jainism, Zoroastrianism, etc. In Buddhism, the yantras, called mandalas, have great importance as they represent the cosmos metaphysically or symbolically.

One of the most famous yantras in Hinduism is the Shri Chakra. Also known as the Wheel of Fortune, this universal yantra represents the entire cosmos. Shri Chakra is also known as Shri Yantra, a complex sacred geometric figure used for worshiping, devotion and meditation. Shri means "wealth," and yantra is loosely translated as "an instrument." The figure has nine interlocking triangles inside a circle, and it symbolizes wish fulfillment. It is encircled by lotus petals inside three circles, and is surrounded by 43 triangles formed by the intersection of the nine triangles. In the eight corners of the square are the eight deities: from clockwise direction—Kubera (North), Ishana (Northeast), Indra (East), Agni (Southeast), Yama (South), Nirrti (Southwest), Varuna (West) and Vaayu (Northwest).

The three outer circles comprise the tattvas: sattva, rajas and tamas.[21] Similarly, the 16 petals of the Shri Yantra are kama or desire, buddhi or intelligence, ahamkara or ego, kaamna or lust, sparsha or touch, roopa or beauty, rasa or taste, gandha or smell, chitta or mind, dhairya or patience, smriti or memory, naam or name, agni or fire, atman or soul, amrita or holy water and himsa or violence. Additionally, the bindu at the center[22] of the Shri Yantra is the point where everything begins—the starting point of life, creation and the universe.

This yantra can also be worshiped every day to remove obstacles from one's life and keep negative energy away. It symbolizes the goddess Shakti through its complex symbology, reflecting the union of the divine feminine and divine masculine. Worshiping the Shri Yantra is viewed as equivalent to honoring Brahman, the highest ultimate force or truth, according to the Tantric sect.[23] Of the different types of Shri Yantra, the most famous are Shri Ganesha Yantra, Lakshmi–Ganesha Yantra, Kubera Yantra and Vishnu Yantra. All these yantras vary in design, yet they all promote prosperity, wealth, good fortune and meditation.

In Hinduism, worshiping the Shri Yantra on Diwali, for the blessings of Lakshmi and Ganesha is considered highly auspicious. Such yantras are predominantly carved into silver, copper and, sometimes, gold. Additionally, these sacred geometries and mystical diagrams are made up of several designs connected with the significant and fundamental elements of the universe. Hence, they not only showcase the comprehensive metaphysical aspects of the universe, but also all the elements that make up the whole of it.

THE FORGOTTEN
ONES

Over thousands of years, Hinduism has diligently preserved a multitude of gods, rituals and festivals. However, in the past two to three centuries, a handful of these cultural elements have faded from collective memory. Some gods and the festivals associated to them, which were once integral to ancient and medieval Hindu practices, have become untraceable today because numerous traditions got lost, especially in the last century. This gradual loss highlights the evolving nature of cultural practices, and the challenges of preserving historical traditions amid modernization and changing social contexts within Hindu communities. Studying forgotten gods can provide valuable insights into the historical and cultural roots of modern Hindu traditions. The captivating stories of these deities, and the symbolism and rituals associated with them can inspire contemporary practices and foster a deeper appreciation for the religion's rich heritage. However, it's essential to approach this study with care, as challenges may arise, including limited or unreliable information and the potential for misinterpretation or conflict with dominant traditions. Being mindful of these factors ensures a respectful and informed exploration of these deities. Some of the forgotten gods from ancient India are:

Alakshmi: She is mentioned in the Padma Purana, with reference to the goddess Nirrti in the Rigveda. Alakshmi was worshiped at dusk, specifically on the day of the new moon in the Kartik month of the Hindu calendar. She is depicted as an elder sister to Lakshmi. Like her, Alakshmi emerged from the cosmic ocean during the churning. But no one was prepared to accept her as Alakshmi was the opposite of Lakshmi; she was associated with the negative aspects of wealth and prosperity and could usher inauspiciousness. Finally, she was assigned the places where bodies were cremated, where people lie and where spouses always fight. In ancient times, people used to worship Alakshmi with devotion; devotees offered food, flowers and incense, particularly during times of hardship or when seeking protection from negative influences. Her worship emphasized the balance between prosperity and adversity, incorporating rites that honored Alakshmi. This was done primarily after cleaning the house, before Lakshmi Puja during Diwali. It was believed that Alakshmi should depart before Lakshmi's arrival. Alakshmi was worshiped with black flowers and brooms. Even today, in some parts of India, it is considered significant to purchase brooms on Diwali.

Lajja Gauri: This lotus-headed goddess, depicted in a birthing posture, is dedicated to the worship of the ancient Devi. She has a lotus head, bent knees and an enlarged belly that indicates childbirth. Hence, she is the goddess of fertility and sexuality. The Lajja Gauri figure is attributed to the call for reproduction. Her worship highlights the significance of motherhood and fertility in Hindu tradition, emphasizing the reverence for the life-giving aspects of the divine.

Gauri refers to "goddess" and lajja means "shame." Lajja signifies her association with modesty and feminine virtues, while Gauri links her to the concept of the divine mother. Together, the name Lajja Gauri embodies the dual aspects of feminine strength and nurturing, highlighting the significance of modesty and motherhood in the realms of fertility and childbirth. However, Lajja Gauri is also known by names like Aditi, Renuka and Kotami. Certain iconography similar to the figure of this goddess are also found in the seals and idols of the Indus Valley civilization. However, the actual representations of Lajja Gauri were seen from the early third century CE, around the reign of the Shunga dynasty. There are various oral and folk tales in rural India about Lajja Gauri that elaborate upon her representation. Unfortunately, Lajja Gauri is only remembered in folklore and legends now.

Madana and Rati: Madana, regarded as the son of Krishna and Rukmini, is also known as an incarnation of Kamadeva. This god was primarily revered in northern India, and some parts of south India during the medieval period. Madana Trayodashi, also known as Madana Utsava or Kama Trayodashi, was the festival that was celebrated for Madana and Rati. Together, they were recognized as the god and goddess of love. The pair was worshiped with flowers, herbs, lyrics and dances in ancient times. In some regions of India, the Madana Trayodashi was also the day devoted to Shiva. There is an interesting story about how Shiva awakened from his meditation, due to the persistence shown by Madana to save the world.

After Sati embraced death by going into the yagna fire, Shiva took to severe meditation for a long time. Eventually, Sati was reborn as Parvati. Parallelly, Indra summoned Madana and told him that the demon king Tarakasura was causing lots of destruction. But only Shiva and his would-be wife, Parvati, could kill this demon. Hence, Indra asked Madana if he could wake Shiva from his penance so that he could marry Parvati. Thereafter, Madana, accompanied by his wife Rati, went to Shiva and tried to rouse him. On being disturbed, he became utterly enraged and immediately incinerated Madana with his third eye. Later, all the gods explained to Shiva that Madana had only come to help them at the request of Indra. Moved by Rati's deep devotion and overwhelming grief for her beloved Madana, Shiva contemplated her unwavering love. Finally, he decided to restore Madana to life, but with a crucial condition—he would no longer possess the same powers as before. As Madana returned to the world, he found himself transformed. While he could still inspire love, his ability to incite uncontrollable desire in others was now limited. This new existence granted him the chance to live alongside Rati and spread love, but with a more measured and thoughtful influence. Their reunion highlighted the importance of love and devotion, showing how love and spiritual focus can coexist in harmony in Hinduism.

Hence, Madana Trayodashi was celebrated on the thirteenth day of the Chaitra Sukla Paksha, to honor the love between a husband and wife. The husbands were supposed to make their wives happy on this auspicious day. This festival is no longer celebrated. It was slowly overtaken or replaced by Holi, which occurs one month before this festival.

As we conclude our exploration of the forgotten gods of Hinduism, we reflect on the diverse spectrum of beliefs and practices that have shaped this ancient religion and its rich traditions. By revisiting these deities and honoring their stories, we deepen our appreciation for the depth and diversity of Hinduism. Acknowledging these forgotten gods keeps their legacies alive, enriching our understanding of devotion, love and the intricate balance of life.

EPILOGUE

Thank you for joining me on this quest for enlightenment as we come to the end of this exploration into the gods of Hinduism. It should now be evident why millions of Hindus worldwide hold these gods and goddesses in such reverence and why they are integral to the people's spiritual journey. Believed to have descended on Earth in various avatars, each deity is honored by Hinduism in all of their forms. Hindus express their devotion through temple visits, idol worship and multiple rituals which start from childhood and continue into adulthood, illustrating the central role of these divine beings in their lives.

Beyond gods, Hinduism encompasses a rich tapestry of rituals, practices, scriptures, ceremonies, cuisine, attire and festivals associated with these multifaceted gods. Each aspect contributes to a vibrant cultural and spiritual heritage that continues to evolve and thrive across generations and continents. Looking ahead, I will explore these aspects and try to reveal the profound wisdom and even deeper insights in my upcoming books.

GLOSSARY

Abhaya Mudra: A powerful hand gesture in Hinduism that symbolizes the granting of protection and safety and the alleviation of fear.

Adityas: A group of solar deities, such as Varuna, Surya, Daksha, who play crucial roles in upholding the cosmic order, protecting humanity and bestowing prosperity on devotees.

Ashtadhyayi: An ancient Sanskrit text on grammar from the fourth century BCE. It consists of eight chapters detailing the rules and structure of Sanskrit grammar.

Atharvademuklaya: A unique type of mantra involving the recitation of two different mantras simultaneously. It is believed to have powerful healing and protective properties, and is often used in Vedic rituals to ward off evil, cure diseases and bring prosperity.

Bindu: Refers to the origin point of the universe, the center point of unmanifested creation, divine and pure potential, and the highest form of consciousness.

Fire sacrifice: A ritual where offerings are made to a sacred fire. It is believed that offerings made to the fire during this sacrifice are carried to the gods and ancestors.

Gopis: The female devotees or cowherd girls of Vrindavan who were deeply in love with Krishna.

Havana: Refers to a Hindu ritualistic yagna or fire ceremony. It involves offering various substances such as ghee, grains, herbs, etc., into a sacred fire, accompanied by the chanting of Vedic mantras.

Itihaas: The historical epics, specifically the Mahabharata and the Ramayana. These texts combine mythology, history, philosophy and moral teachings, presenting narratives that are integral to Hindu culture and tradition.

Jnanakanda: Refers to the philosophical and spiritual aspects of the Vedic religion, emphasizing spiritual knowledge, self-realization and liberation from the cycle of birth and death.

Karmakanda: A term that refers to the ritualistic and ceremonial aspects of Vedic religion. It encompasses sacrifices, rituals and sacraments. Its primary goal is to maintain the order of the universe, ensure individual and societal well-being, and help people attain spiritual merit, prosperity, happiness and, ultimately, liberation.

Kartal: Refers to a percussion instrument commonly used in devotional music, particularly in bhajans or devotional songs, and kirtans or devotional chants.

Lord Ardhanarishwara: A unique form of Shiva depicted as half-man and half-woman, symbolizing the synthesis of masculine and feminine energies.

Lord Panchamukhalinga: The five-faced linga; Shiva's five faces represent the traditional elements, directions, senses and body parts. Sadyojata, Vamadeva, Aghora, Tatpurusha and Ishana are Shiva's five aspects that relate to the classical elements and the cardinal directions.

Moksha: Refers to liberation or release from samsara or the cycle of birth and death. It is the ultimate goal of the soul, representing its union with the divine, and freedom from all earthly attachments and suffering.

Navagraha: Refers to the nine celestial bodies that are significant in Hindu astrology and worship. These include Surya or sun, Chandra or moon, Mangala or Mars, Budha or Mercury, Brihaspati or Jupiter, Shukra or Venus, Shani or Saturn, Rahu or North Lunar Node and Ketu or South Lunar Node.

Parmatman: In Hinduism, Parmatman is a core belief that refers to the Supreme Self or Absolute Atman, which is also known as the "Primordial Self."

Rudras: Represents a group of powerful deities associated with both the destructive and healing aspects of nature.

Samudra Manthan: A well-known tale chronicled in the Puranas. The narrative revolves around the devas and asuras or demons, in pursuit of Amrita or the nectar of immortality. Unable to attain it individually, both groups decided to collaborate in churning the Ksheera Sagara or the ocean of milk with the aim of procuring the coveted nectar.

Sanatan Dharma: Denotes the duties and ordained practices followed by Hinduism, regardless of class, caste or sect.

Shakti Peetha: Sacred shrines dedicated to the worship of Shakti in her various forms. The exact number of Shakti Peethas varies across traditions, with different texts listing 51–108 peethas. They are spread across the Indian subcontinent, in countries including India, Bangladesh, Nepal, Pakistan and Sri Lanka.

Shankha: A conch shell, which holds immense significance in Hinduism and is revered as sacred and auspicious. It symbolizes the primordial sound of creation, "aum," which is believed to resonate throughout the universe.

Shri Yantra: An important device used in the worship of the primordial energy, which is the cause for the creation, maintenance and destruction of the cosmos.

Suktas: Refers to hymns or poetic compositions found in the Vedic texts. These hymns are composed in a structured meter and are dedicated to various deities. They express praise, invocation and spiritual insights.

Upavedas: Subsidiary texts that came alongside the main Vedas in ancient India. They focus on practical knowledge and other specialized fields derived from Vedic teachings. There are four Upavedas linked to each of the main Vedas: Ayurveda (from the Rigveda) deals with health and medicine; Dhanurveda (from the Yajurveda) covers martial arts and weaponry; Gandharvaveda (from the Samaveda) involves music, dance and the arts; and Arthaveda (from the Atharvaveda) discusses economics, governance and politics.

Vajra: A legendary and ritualistic weapon, symbolizing the indestructability of a diamond and the incredible strength of a thunderbolt.

Vastu Shastra: The ancient Hindu science of architecture and design. It focuses on designing spaces in harmony with natural forces, cosmic energies and the environment.

Vasus: A group of eight deities associated with natural elements and phenomena. They are considered attendants of Indra and are revered in various Vedic hymns for their role in maintaining the natural order.

Vedangas: Six additional subjects, developed to help people understand, chant and use the Vedas better. These subjects cover shiksha (phonetics), kalpa (rituals), vyakarana (grammar), nirukta (word meanings), chandas (meter) and jyotisha (astronomy). They provide essential tools for correctly chanting and understanding Vedic texts, performing rituals accurately, interpreting knowledge about heavenly bodies and exploring the language mentioned in the Vedas.

Vishvedevas: Often mentioned in Vedic literature, including the Rigveda, alongside other groups of deities like the Adityas or sons of Aditi, Maruts or storm gods and Vasus or attendant gods. They are understood to embody the divine forces governing different aspects of existence, such as natural phenomena, celestial bodies and cosmic principles.

Yamadutas: The messengers or servants of Yama; they are the beings responsible for escorting souls from the mortal world to the afterlife, specifically to Yamloka or Yama's realm.

REFERENCES

1. Kak, Subhash, "On the Chronological Framework for Indian Culture," Indian Council of Philosophical Research (2000).

2. Mathpal, Yashodhar, *Prehistoric Painting of Bhimbetka* (India: Abhinav Publications, 1984).

3. Kak, Subhash, *The Astronomical Code of the Rigveda* (India: Aditya Prakashan, 2020).

4. Regional Remote Sensing Centre, NRSC/ISRO, Department of Space, Govt. of India, "River Saraswati: An Integrated Study Based on Remote Sensing & GIS Techniques with Ground Information" (2014).

5. Durant, Will, *The Story of Philosophy* (United States: Simon & Schuster, 1926).

6. Arya Samaj Gandhidham, "The Vedic Conception of God." https://www.aryagan.org/pdf/literature/ved/Vedic-Conception-of-God.pdf

7. Saraswati, Sri Chandrasekharendra, *The Vedas* (India: Bhavan's Book University, 2016).

8. *The Vishnu Purana.* Translated by Horace Hayman Wilson (1840). sacred-texts.comhttps://sacred-texts.com/hin//vp/vp077.htm

9. "Swami Vivekananda and His 1893 Speech," *Art Institute of Chicago*, accessed July 6, 2024. https://www.artic.edu/swami-vivekananda-and-his-1893-speech.

10. Bhattacharyya, Ashim Kumar, *Hindu Dharma: Introduction to Scriptures and Theology* (iUniverse, 2006).

11. Surendranath Dasgupta, *A History of Indian Philosophy* (Cambridge University Press, 2009); Roshen Dalal, *The Vedas: An Introduction to Hinduism's Sacred Texts* (India: Penguin, 2014); S. Radhakrishnan, *The Principal Upanisads* (United Kingdom: HarperCollins, 2006).

12. Talageri, Shrikant G., *The Rigveda: A Historical Analysis* (India: Aditya Prakashan, 2000).

13. United Nations Educational, Scientific and Cultural Organization (UNESCO), *Proclamation of the Masterpieces of the Oral and Intangible Heritage of Humanity* (UNESCO, 2001–2005).

14. Ganatra, Ami, *Mahabharata Unravelled: Lesser-Known Facets of a Well-Known History* (India: Bloomsbury India, 2021).

15. Vyasa, Krishna-Dwaipayana, *The Mahabharata of Krishna-Dwaipayana Vyasa Book 1 Adi Parva* (India: Spastic Cat Press, 2013).

16. Pravase, "History, Importance, Timings, Festivals, Architecture, Activities, Interesting Facts and Travel Guide of Shri Trinetra Ganesh Temple, Ranthambore, Rajasthan, India". https://pravase.co.in/thingstododetail/657/india/rajasthan/ranthambore/trinetra-ganesh-temple-ranthambore-fort-timing-history-importance-architecture-tourist-guide

17. "Swastika Is Pre-Aryan Invasion, if Any; Dates Back 11000 Years in Vedic India: Evidences & Explorations," IIT-Kharagpur, Indian Council of Cultural Relations (ICCR). https://iitkgpsandhi.org/Swastika_Monograph%202016.pdf

18. Nikhilananda, Swami, *The Mandukya Upanishad* (India: Advaita Ashram, 2006).

19. "Kalyani B.G., G. Venkatasubramanian, R. Arasappa, N.P. Rao, S.V. Kalmady, R.V. Behere, H. Rao, M.K. Vasudev, B.N. Gangadhar, Neurohemodynamic correlates of 'OM' chanting: A pilot functional magnetic resonance imaging study," *The National Library of Medicine: National Center for Biotechnology Information* (2011). https://www.ncbi.nlm.nih.gov/pmc/articles/PMC3099099/

20. Avalon, Arthur, *Shakti and Shakta* (Dover Publications, 1918).

21. Widgery, Alban G., "The Principles of Hindu Ethics," *International Journal of Ethics* 40, no. 2 (1930).

22. Kuiper, Kathleen, *The Culture of India* (Britannica Educational Pub, 2010).

23. Rao, S.K. Ramachandra, *Sri-Chakra: Its Yantra, Mantra and Tantra* (India: Sri Satguru Publications, 2008).

FURTHER READINGS

- Chatterjee, Anirban, Jyotiranjan S. Ray, Anil D. Shukla and Kanchan Pande. "On the Existence of a Perennial River in the Harappan Heartland." Scientific Reports, 2019. https://www.nature.com/articles/s41598-019-53489-4

- Das, Sisir Kumar. *A History of Indian Literature, 500-1399: From Courtly to the Popular.* Sahitya Akademi Publications, 2005.

- *Dwadesh Jyotirling.* Gorakhpur: Gita Press.

- Garg, Acharya Krishna Kumar. *Stories from Vedas.* 2019.

- Goswami, Tulsidas. *Ramcharitmanas.* Gorakhpur: Gita Press, 2018.

- Iyengar, T.R.R. *Dictionary of Hindu Gods and Goddesses.* 2003.

- Jennings, Hargrave. *Nature Worship an Account of Phallic Faith and Practices.* Fredonia Books, 2001.

- Kak, Subhash. "The Mahabharata and the Sindhu-Sarasvati Tradition." https://www.ece.lsu.edu/kak/MahabharataII.pdf

- Martin, E. Osborn. *The Gods of India: A Brief Description of Their History, Character and Worship.* 1914.

- Doniger, Wendy, Merriam-Webster, Inc. *Merriam-Webster's Encyclopedia of World Religions*. Merriam Webster, 1999.
- Paranjape, Makarand. *Swami Vivekananda: Hinduism and India's Road to Modernity*. India: HarperCollins, 2019.
- Parmanand, Yug Purush Swami. *Mandukya Upanishad: Series II: The True Method of Self-realization*. 2002.
- Prasoon, Shrikant. *Eternal Human Religion-Hinduism Clarified and Simplified*. V&S Publishers, 2011.
- Paramananda, Swami. *The Upanishads*, trans. 2020.
- Tapasyananda, Swami. *Bhakti Schools of Vedanta*. Sri Ramakrishna Math, 1990.
- Translated by Manmatha Nath Dutt. *The Ramayana by Valmiki: Ayodhya Kandam*. 1892.
- V.S. Rao. *Navagraha Purana,* ed. Preetha Rajah Kannan. India: Jaico Publishing House, 2016.
- Vishnuswaroop, Swami. *Shiva Samhita: A Classical Text on Yoga and Tantra*. 2002.
- Wilson, Horace Hayman. *Rig-Veda-Sanhita: A Collection of Ancient Hindu Hymns*. 1857.
- Wood, Ananda. *From the Upanishads*. Zen Publications, 1996.
- Zimmer, Heinrich Robert. *Myths and Symbols in Indian Art and Civilization*. Princeton University Press, 1962.

ACKNOWLEDGMENTS

I am profoundly grateful to all who have supported me on this journey. In memory of my beloved mother, whose love and wisdom continue to illuminate my path, I dedicate this work. My father's unwavering support has been instrumental in shaping my character. To my wife and children, whose love and encouragement have been my constant source of strength, I express my heartfelt gratitude. To my sister and brother, whose companionship and support have enriched my life, I am eternally thankful. This book is a testament to the collective efforts of all those who have believed in me and this project.

ABOUT THE AUTHOR

Manhar Sharma, an engineer and author, is deeply passionate about researching Hinduism and Vedic literature. He holds a master's degree in computer science and has dedicated nearly a decade to studying Indian scriptures. His extensive exploration has led to the publication of many articles focusing on religious scriptures, Hinduism and the Vedas. Through his writings, Manhar strives to bridge the ancient wisdom of Vedic texts with contemporary understanding, aiming to illuminate the deep insights and cultural richness found within Hindu traditions.